# Priscilla Hauser's
## DECORATIVE PAINTING
# WORKSHOP

# Priscilla Hauser's
## DECORATIVE PAINTING
# WORKSHOP

Priscilla Hauser

## Sterling Publishing Co., Inc.
New York

Prolific Impressions Production Staff:

Editor in Chief: Mickey Baskett
Copy Editor: Phyllis Mueller
Graphics: Dianne Miller, Karen Turpin
Styling: Lenos Key
Photography: Jerry Mucklow, Steve Wilcox
Administration: Jim Baskett

Published by Sterling Publishing Co., Inc.
387 Park Avenue South, New York, N.Y. 10016

© 2005 by Prolific Impressions, Inc.
Produced by Prolific Impressions, Inc.
160 South Candler St., Decatur, GA 30030

Distributed in Canada by Sterling Publishing
c/o Canadian Manda Group, 165 Dufferin Street
Toronto , Ontario, Canada M6K 3H6
Distributed in Great Britain by Chrysalis Books Group PLC,
The Chrysalis Building, Bramley Road, London W10 6SP, England
Distributed in Australia by Capricorn Link (Australia) Pty. Ltd.
P.O. Box 704, Windsor, NSW 2756 Australia

Printed in the U.S.A
All rights reserved
Sterling ISBN 1-4027-1477-7

Acknowledgements
Thank you to the following manufacturers for supplying the products to complete the projects in this book.

*For wood surfaces:* Walnut Hollow, 1409 State Road 23 Dodgeville, WI 53533-2112, 800-395-5995

*For brushes:* Kala Brush Company, info@kalabrush.com, 580-657-6605

*For paints:* Plaid Enterprises, Inc., www.plaidonline.com

*For etching compound:* B & B Etching, 17921 N. 98th Ave., Peoria, AZ 85382, 888-382-4255, etchall@etchall.com

*For china lamp, tile trivets, china vase:* Mr. & Mrs. of Dallas, 800-878-7528, www.dallaschina.com

*For canvas bag:* BagWorks, info@bagworks.com, 800-678-7364

# About the Artist

She's the "First Lady of Decorative Painting," and with good reason. Due to Priscilla's efforts, dreams, and ability to draw people to her, the first meeting of the National Society of Tole & Decorative Painters took place on October 22, 1972 with 21 other people attending. Since then the organization has thrived, and so has Priscilla.

From Priscilla's beginning efforts as a tole painter in the early 1960s, having taken tole painting classes at a YMCA in Raytown, MO, she has become a world renowned teacher, author, and the decorative painting industry's ambassador to the world. She has used nearly every outlet to share her enthusiasm for and knowledge of decorative painting. Besides teaching all over the

world, Priscilla has illustrated her technique through books, magazine articles, videos, and television. The results of her teaching method have lead to an accreditation program for teachers. She has traveled to teach in Canada, Japan, Argentina, and The Netherlands, as well as extensive teaching within the United States at her "Studio by the Sea" in Panama City Beach, Florida.

For information about Priscilla Hauser Painting Seminars,
you can contact Priscilla as follows:
Priscilla Hauser
P.O. Box 521013, Tulsa, OK 74152
Fax: (918) 743-5075
Phone: (918) 743-6072
Website: www.priscillahuaser.com
email: phauser376@aol.com

## DEDICATION

Dedicated with love to my paint team, my dream team, the creative women who are always there for me and make me look good—Judy Kimball, Naomi Meeks, Sue Sensintaffar, Joyce Beebe, Barbara Saunders, and Janet Alphin.
I couldn't do it without you.

# TABLE OF

# CONTENTS

PAGE 68

PAGE 84

PAGE 98

PAGE 106

When you learn to paint, your horizons magically expand
into a world of color and creation. Decorative painting is as
easy as "A B C", but it takes practice and determination to
learn the essentials. When you do, the joys of painting
are yours forever.

I encourage you to start by working on your skills.
(I know you want to get to the projects, but first it's
important to learn the skills and understand the terminology.)
Diligently practice and learn how paint works. Learn the
proper application of paint on different surfaces, and what
types of paint yield good results.

In this book you'll see how to apply the essentials—
basic brush strokes, floating, and blending—while painting
different motifs on a variety of surfaces, including wood, metal,
glass, ceramics, fabric, and paper. Complete each lesson at least
three times before painting it on a project.

*Priscilla Hauser*

Decorative
painting is as
easy as
"A B C"...

# ABOUT ACRYLIC PAINTS

There are marvelous acrylic paints for painting on all kinds of surfaces. It's important to choose the right paint for the surface. Cleanup is easy with soap and water.

**Wood, Fabric, Paper, Candles:**

Many of the projects in this book, including wood, fabric, and paper surfaces, were painted with **artist pigment acrylics**. These rich, creamy, opaque paints come in squeeze bottles and are available at art supply and craft stores. They have true pigment color names, just like oil paints. Their pigment is brilliant, and you can blend them and move them much in the same way as oil paints by using painting mediums.

Pre-mixed **acrylic craft paints** are available in hundreds of colors. These are not true pigment colors, but blended colors. They have the same consistency as artist pigment acrylics and can be used for decorative painting the same way as artist pigment acrylics. In this book, I use them to undercoat designs and for basecoating. If you choose paints from the same manufacturer, you can be sure they will be compatible with one another.

**Glass & Ceramics:**

To paint on glass and ceramic surfaces, you'll want to use **acrylic enamels**, which are specially formulated to perform well on shiny and slick surfaces. These paints require no special preparation and are self-sealing and scratch-resistant. They can be air dried to cure or baked in a home oven for added durability.

**Outdoor Surfaces:**

To paint on surfaces that you wish to use outdoors such as metal watering cans, clay pots, and tiles, choose an **outdoor enamel** paint. No sealing will be necessary and they will hold up well in the weather.

**Paper:**

For painting on paper, you can use artist pigment acrylics and acrylic paints or choose an acrylic **paper paint**. These paints are acid-free and can be used for dimensional, textured, or flat finishes. They are available in satin, metallic, and glitter sheens, but the range of colors is much

## Painting Mediums

Mediums are liquids or gels that are mixed with paint for achieving specific effects. They are sold along with acrylic paints. It's always best to use mediums and paints from the same manufacturer.

### Mediums for Artist Pigment Acrylics

**Floating medium** is used to thin the paint so that it can be used for floating a color. The brush is filled with the floating medium, and a corner of the brush is then filled with color. After the brush is blended on the palette, the color is brushed along the edge of a design element to create a shading or highlighting.

**Blending medium** is used to keep paint wet and moving. The medium is painted on the surface in the area of the design where you're painting, and the design is painted immediately while the blending medium is still wet.

**Glazing medium** is used to thin the paint so the mixture can be used for antiquing or to create transparent textured effects. The glazing medium is mixed with the paint on a palette or in a small container until a transparent consistency is reached. This medium can also be used as a substitute for

floating medium. It works in the same way.

**Textile medium** is mixed with paint before the paint is applied to cloth. The paint will be permanent on the fabric when it dries.

**Water** can also be considered a medium. It thins paint for line work and washes.'

### Mediums for Acrylic Enamels

You don't want to use water to thin acrylic enamels. Always use the painting mediums specially manufactured for the paint you're using.

**Clear medium** works much like floating medium—it gives the paint a transparent quality.

**Flow medium** helps paint flow off the brush so it's helpful when painting line work or details.

**Extender** works like a blending medium. It gives the paint more open time, so you have more time to work the paint before it dries.

## Mediums for Paper Paints

To use paper paints for brush work, you'll need to use a **flow medium** to thin the paint to the proper consistency.

### HINTS FROM PRISCILLA

- Acrylic paints like to be cold. They won't dry as quickly if the room temperature is 68 degrees or colder. Heat dries, cold does not.

- Do not allow air to blow on your project while you're painting. Rapidly moving air dries the paint. Still air allows you more time to move the paint.

- Humidity keeps things wet. The higher the humidity, the more time you'll have for blending.

- Use a lot of paint so the colors will blend together.

*My work area, ready for painting!*

# ABOUT BRUSHES

There are many different types of brushes, and different-shaped brushes do different things. You will need four types of brushes in various sizes to do your decorative painting. The individual project instructions list the sizes of brushes needed for that particular project.

## FLAT BRUSHES

Flat brushes are designed for brush strokes and blending. These brushes do most of the painting of the designs.

## ROUND BRUSHES

Round brushes are used primarily for stroking—we seldom blend with them. They can also be used for some detail work.

## FILBERT BRUSHES

Filbert brushes are a cross between a flat and a round brush. They are generally used for stroking, but can also be used for blending.

## LINER BRUSHES

Liner brushes are very thin round brushes that come to a wonderful point. Good liner brushes are needed for fine line work.

When it comes to brushes, please purchase the very best that money can buy. They are your tools—the things you paint with. Occasionally, a student says, "Priscilla, I don't want to buy a good brush until I know I can paint." I always tell my students they won't be able to paint if they don't begin with a good brush. You get what you pay for.

Brush strokes are the basis of my decorative painting technique. This book includes excellent brush stroke worksheets for practicing. To use them, lay a sheet of acetate or tracing paper over the top of the worksheet, choose a brush approximately the same size as the brush used on the worksheet, and practice hundreds of strokes on top of mine. (If a hundred sounds like a lot, get over it! You will find that painting a hundred strokes happens very quickly.)

## Other Paint Applicators

- **Sponge brushes** can be used for basecoating and for applying varnish. These are usually 1" wide and inexpensive.
- **Stencil brushes** can be used to pounce or dab paint on surfaces.
- Round **sponge-on-a-stick applicators** are great for painting circular design motifs—you can find them in a variety of sizes. Smaller ones may be labeled "**daubers**."

## BRUSH CARE

It's important to clean your brushes properly and keep them in excellent condition. To thoroughly clean them:

1. Gently flip-flop each brush back and forth in water until all the paint is removed, rinsing them thoroughly. Never slam brushes into a container and stir them.

2. Work brush cleaner through the hairs of the brush in a small dish and wipe the brush on a soft, absorbent rag. Continue cleaning until there is no trace of color on the rag.
3. Shape the brush with your fingers and store it so nothing can distort the shape of the hairs. Rinse the brush in water before using again.

Brush types, *pictured left to right*: Round, filbert, liner, flat.

# BASIC PAINTING SUPPLIES

In addition to paint, mediums, and brushes, these are basic painting supplies that are needed for each project. They are not listed in the individual project instructions; you will, however, need to gather them for each and every project.

**Tracing Paper** - I like to use a very thin, transparent tracing paper for tracing designs. I use a **pencil** for tracing.

**Brown Paper Bags** - I use pieces of brown paper bags with no printing on them to smooth surfaces after basecoating and between coats of varnish.

**Chalk, White and Colored** - I use chalk for transferring the traced design to the prepared painting surface. Because chalk will easily wipe away and not show through the paint, I prefer it to graphite paper. Do not buy the dustless kind of chalk. I also use a **charcoal pencil** for transferring some designs.

**Graphite Transfer Paper** - Occasionally, I use white or gray graphite paper to transfer my design. However, I try to avoid using it because the lines may show through the paint. It can also make smudges on the background that are not easily removed.

**Stylus** - Use a stylus tool for transferring your traced design to the prepared surface. A pencil or a ballpoint pen that no longer writes also may be used.

**Palette** - I like to use a "stay-wet" type palette. Some people prefer a wax-coated or dry palette for acrylics; however, I prefer a palette that stays wet since acrylics dry so quickly. A wet palette consists of a plastic tray that holds a wet sponge and special paper. Palettes can be found where decorative painting supplies are sold.

**Palette Knife** - Use a palette knife for mixing and moving paint on your palette or mixing surface. I prefer a straight-blade palette knife made of flexible steel.

**100% Cotton Rags** - Use only 100% cotton rags for wiping your brush. *Try the knuckle test: For 15 seconds, rub your knuckles on the rag that you wipe your brush on. If your knuckles bleed, think of what that rag is doing to the hairs of your brush!* You could also use soft, absorbent **paper towels** for wiping brushes.

**Water Basin:** Use a water basin or other container filled with water for rinsing brushes.

**Varnish:** See "Finishing Your Piece" for details.

*For projects on wood:*

**Sandpaper** - I use sandpaper for smoothing unfinished and finished wood surfaces and for creating a distressed, aged look on painted surfaces. Sandpaper comes in various grades from very fine to very coarse. It's good to keep a supply on hand.

**Tack Cloth** - A tack rag or tack cloth is a piece of cheesecloth or other soft cloth that has been treated with a mixture of varnish and linseed oil. It is very sticky. Use it for wiping a freshly sanded surface to remove all dust particles. When not in use, store the tack rag in a tightly sealed jar.

**Wood Filler** - Choose a good wood filler for filling holes, knots, and cracks. Follow the manufacturer's instructions for application.

## USING A WET PALETTE

A wet palette consists of a plastic tray that holds a wet sponge and special paper. To use this type of palette:

1. Soak the sponge in water until saturated. Do not wring out, but place the very wet sponge into the tray. (Photo 1)

2. Soak the paper that comes with the palette in water for 12-24 hours. Place the paper on top of the very wet sponge. (Photo 2)

3. Wipe the surface of the paper with a soft, absorbent rag to remove the excess water. (Photo 3)

4. Squeeze paint on the palette. When paints are placed on top of a properly prepared wet palette, they will stay wet for a long time. (Photo 4)

**Photo 2**

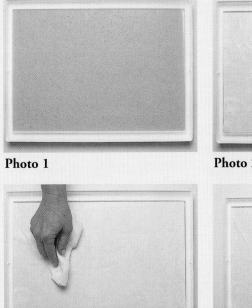

**Photo 1**

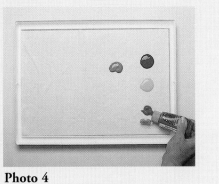

**Photo 3**

**Photo 4**

# PAINTING TERMS

### Basecoating

Preparing and painting your project surface before the decorative painting is applied is called basecoating.

### Basic Brush Strokes

Basic brush strokes are done with round and flat brushes. Brush strokes are like the letters of the alphabet. They are easy to learn, but they do require practice. Learning them is very important as they are the basis for all of your painting. For example, if you are painting a flower petal, such as a daisy, you will paint each petal with one brush stroke such as a teardrop. Use as few strokes as possible to paint each part of the design.

### Color Wash

A color wash is an application of very thin paint. Actually, one could say it is water with just a little color in it that is applied over a painted surface to add a blush of color. A wash can also be made with glazing medium and a bit of color.

### Consistency

Consistency describes the thickness or thinness of the paint. You need different consistencies for different techniques. When you do brush strokes, the paint must be a creamy consistency. When you do line work, the paint must be very thin like the consistency of ink. If the paint is too thick, add a few drops of water to the paint puddle on your palette and mix with a palette knife until the proper consistency is reached.

### Contrast

Contrast is the sharp difference between two or more colors. When two colors meet, one edge must be light (usually the top edge) and the other edge or shadowed area must be dark. Contrast gives life to your painting.

### Curing

When something is dry to the touch, it is not cured. If something is cured, it is dry all the way through. I often

*Continued on next page*

15

explain curing with this analogy: If you fall down and skin your knee and it bleeds, it's wet. When the scab forms, it's dry. When the new skin grows, it's cured.

I am frequently asked how long it takes a painted piece to cure. There is no right answer—curing depends upon the temperature, air circulation, humidity, the paint color used, and the thinness or thickness of the paint. When a piece is cured, it feels warm and dry to the touch. Curing can take three hours or several weeks.

## Double-Loading

Double-loading is a technique of loading the brush with two colors of paint. Using two different puddles of paint, load half of the brush with the lighter color and the other half with the darker color. Blend by stroking your brush many, many times on the palette on one side of the brush, then turn the brush over and stroke on the other side. It takes many strokes to prime a brush and get it good and full of paint.

## Outlining

Most of the time, I outline with a #1 liner brush. (It's possible to outline with the very fine point of any good brush.) When outlining, the brush should be full of paint that has been thinned to the consistency of ink.

## Stippling

To stipple, you need a brush with a flat tip—a stippling brush, a scruffy brush, or a stencil brush. The brush is loaded, then dabbed up and down on the surface to produce an irregular covering of paint—little dots or specks—from the flat brush tip.

## Undercoating

Undercoating is neatly and smoothly painting a design or part of a design solidly on the basecoated project surface. Your strokes, shading, and highlighting will be done on top of this undercoated design.

## Wash

See "Color Wash."

# USING A FLAT BRUSH

Flat brushes are designed for brush strokes and blending. They come in many different sizes. Flat brush strokes or any type of stroke may be painted in a single color. It is always a good idea to practice the stroke using a single color before you double-load. These photos show a double-loaded brush, but the procedure is the same if you are using a single color. Practice your flat brush strokes on the Brush Stroke Worksheet that follows.

## Double-Loading

Double-loading involves loading your brush with two colors. Be sure to thin the paint with water to a flowing consistency and push it with a palette knife to form a neat puddle with a clean edge.

**Photo 1.** Stroke up against the edge of the light color 30 times, so half of the brush is loaded with paint and the other half is clean.

*Double Loading, continued*

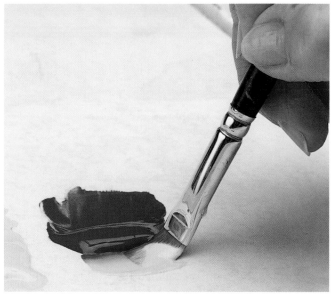

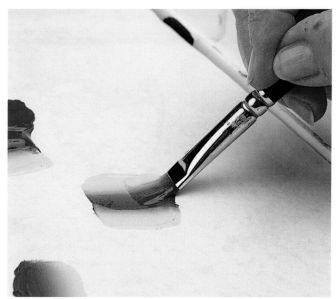

**Photo 2.** Turn the brush over and stroke up against the edge of the dark color 20 times.

**Photo 3.** Blend, blend, blend one side of the brush on your palette. Turn the brush over and blend, blend, blend on the other side, keeping the dark color in the center and the light color to the outside. Pick up more light paint on the brush and blend some more. Pick up more of the dark color and blend some more. Continue doing this until your brush is really full with paint. You don't want a space between the two colors; you want them to blend into each other in the center of the brush.

## Basic Stroke

## Line Stroke

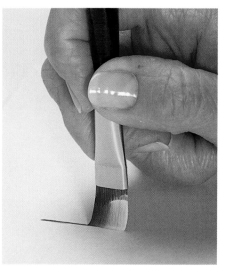

**Photo 1.** Touch the length of the flat or chisel edge of the brush to your surface.

**Photo 2.** Press the brush down and pull it toward you, holding the pressure steady. Lift the brush smoothly at the end of the stroke.

Stand the brush on its flat or chisel edge, perpendicular to the orientation of the basic flat stroke. The handle should point straight up toward the ceiling. Pull the brush toward you. Don't press the brush down, as this would thicken and distort the line.

# USING A ROUND BRUSH

Round brushes are used primarily for stroking—we seldom blend with them. They come in a variety of sizes. Practice your round brush strokes on the Brush Stroke Worksheet.

## Loading the Brush

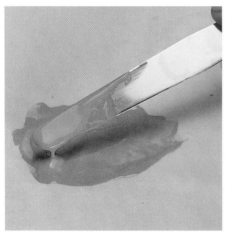

**Photo 1.** Squeeze paint on your palette. If needed, thin your paint with a thinning medium such as glazing medium or water. Paint should be a creamy consistency.

**Photo 2.** Load brush by picking up paint from the edge of the puddle.

## Teardrop or Polliwog Stroke

**Photo 1.** Touch on the tip of the brush and apply pressure.

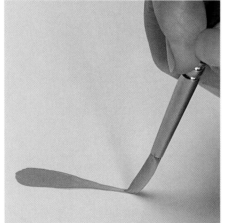

**Photo 2.** Gradually lift and drag straight down. Turning the brush slightly left or right forces the hairs back together to form a point.

# USING A LINER BRUSH

Liner brushes are the long, thinner members of the round brush family. Their bristles come to a wonderful point. Liner brushes are used for fine line work. Practice your liner brush strokes on the Brush Stroke Worksheet.

## Loading the Brush

## Teardrop Stroke

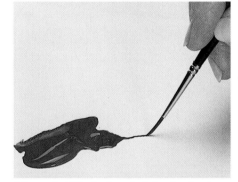

**Photo 1.** Thin paint with water until it is the consistency of ink.

**Photo 2.** Fill the brush full of paint by pulling it through paint puddle edge. Twist the brush as you pull it out of puddle (this will form a nice pointed tip). When you are using the brush hold it straight up.

Fill brush with paint of a thin consistency; touch, apply pressure, begin pulling and lifting, then drag to a point.

## Curlicues & Squiggles

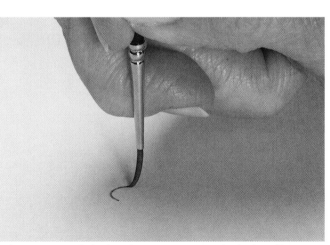

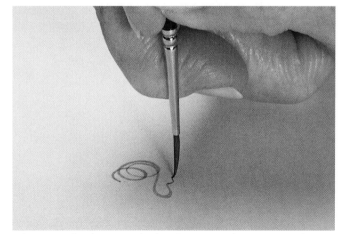

**Photo 1.** Stand the brush on its point with the handle pointing straight up toward the ceiling.

**Photo 2.** Slowly move the brush to paint loopy Ms and Ws. Practice several times on your page. Make as many variations as you wish.

# BRUSH STROKE WORKSHEET

## Round Brush Strokes

Comma      Comma left      Comma Right

## Filbert Brush Strokes

Comma, Left      Comma, Right      Comma

## Flat Brush Strokes

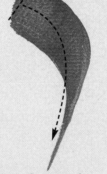

Basic      Line      Comma left      Comma right      U-Strokes

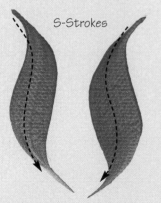

S-Strokes

Half Circle Strokes

## Double-Loaded Brush Strokes (using a #12 flat brush)

Basic

Line

Comma left

Comma right

U-Strokes

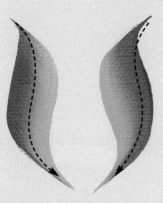

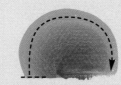

S-Strokes

Half Circle Strokes

## Liner Brush Strokes

Use a very thin paint and a full brush. Move the brush slowly.

Polliwog

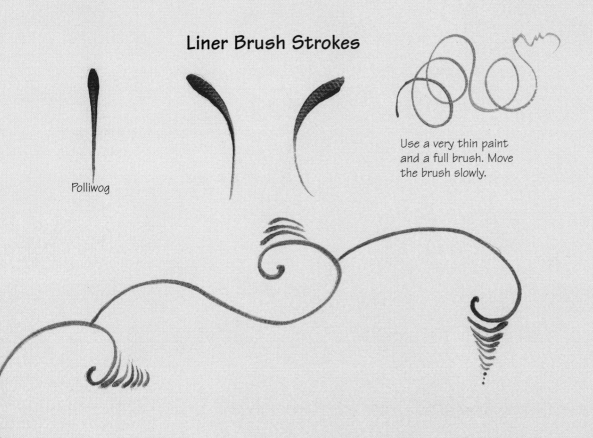

# PAINTING TECHNIQUES

## Shading & Highlighting with Floating

Floating is flowing color on a surface. This technique is used for adding the shading and highlighting to design elements. Before floating, undercoat the area using the medium tone color of the design. Let dry. Add a second or even a third coat, if necessary. Let dry. Our example shows shading and highlighting floated on a leaf that has been undercoated in a gray-green (bayberry) color.

**Photo 1.** Fill your brush with floating medium. Your brush size is determined by the design.

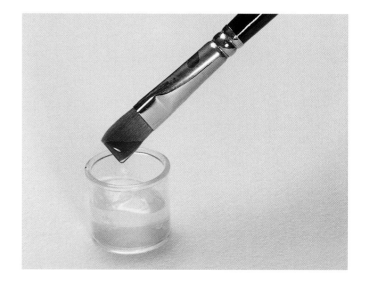

**Photo 2.** Fill one side of the brush with the shading color by stroking up against the edge of a puddle of paint.

**Photo 3.** On a matte surface, such as tracing paper or wet palette paper, blend, blend, blend on one side of the brush.

**Photo 4.** Then turn the brush over and blend, blend, blend on the other side. Keep the paint in the center. Be sure the brush is good and full of paint and that the color graduates through the brush from dark to medium to clear.

**Photo 5.** The floating of shading and highlighting will be done atop the undercoating. Here the leaf was undercoated with bayberry.

**Photo 6.** Float on the shading to the edge of the design (here, a leaf), with the dark side of the brush towards the outside of the design. Let dry. Repeat the process, if desired, to deepen the color.

*Shading & Highlighting, continued*

**Photo 7.** Highlighting is floated on the opposite side of the design, using the same technique as shading but using a light color.

*Option:* Water can be used in place of floating medium. Dip the brush in water and blot by gently pulling the brush along the edge of your water basin.

# Blending

In this book, I have done a very easy type of blending. First, neatly and carefully undercoat and let dry. Blending medium, which allows you to easily blend colors together, is painted onto design area that you want to blend.

**Photo 1.** Float on the shadows. Let dry.

**Photo 2.** Add a small amount of blending medium to area of design where you will be blending color.

**Photo 3.** Add the colors you wish to blend on top of the wet medium.

**Photo 4.** Lightly blend or move the colors together, using an extremely light touch. If you are heavy handed, you will wipe all the color away. If this happens, let the blending medium dry and cure and begin again *or* remove the color before it dries, add more blending medium, and begin again.

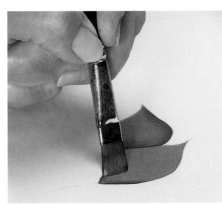

**Photo 1**

**Photo 2**

**Photo 3**

**Photo 4**

# BASIC INFORMATION

## Transferring Patterns

### Transferring a Design with Transfer Paper

It is fine to transfer designs to a surface with white or gray transfer paper; however, this is my least favorite way to transfer a design because transfer paper tends to smudge. Here's how to use transfer paper:

1. Trace the pattern neatly and carefully from the book on tracing paper, using a pencil or fine point marker.
2. Position tracing on surface. Secure with tape.
3. Slide the transfer paper under the tracing with the transfer side facing the surface.
4. Using a stylus, neatly trace over the pattern lines to transfer the lines to the surface.

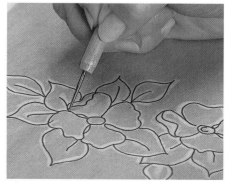

### Transferring with a Charcoal Pencil

1. Neatly trace the pattern of the design onto tracing paper. You may use a pencil or a pen.
2. Turn over the traced design. Firmly go over the traced lines on the back with a charcoal pencil. (Photo 1)
3. Position the design on the prepared surface, charcoal side down. Using a stylus, go over the lines. (Photo 2)

Don't press so hard that you make indentations in the surface. The pattern lines will be transferred to your surface.

**Photo 1**

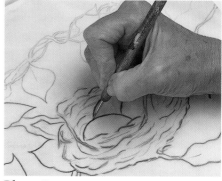

**Photo 2**

### Transferring with Chalk

1. Neatly trace the pattern of the design onto tracing paper. You may use a pencil or a pen. It is not necessary to trace shading lines or curlicues.
2. Turn over the traced design. Firmly go over the traced lines on the back with chalk. (Photo 1) Do not scribble all over the tracing with the chalk.
3. Shake off the excess chalk dust, being careful not to inhale the particles.
4. Position the design on the prepared surface, chalk side down. Using a stylus, go over the lines. (Photo 2) Don't press so hard that you make indentations in the surface. The chalk will be transferred to your surface. Chalk is easily removed and it dissolves as you paint over it.

**Photo 1**

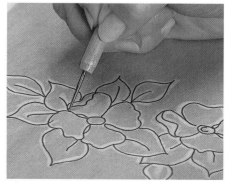

**Photo 2**

# Flyspecking

Flyspecking adds an aged look to your pieces. To flyspeck, you need an old **toothbrush**, the **paint** color of your choice, **glazing medium**, a **palette knife**, and a mixing surface such as a **palette** or a **plastic container**.

1. Place a small amount of the paint color on your mixing surface. Add glazing medium to paint, Mix with a palette knife to a very thin consistency. The thinner the paint, the finer the spatter. Thicker paint makes larger spatters.
2. Dip the toothbrush in the thinned paint. (Photo 1)
3. Point the toothbrush at your surface and pull your thumb across the bristles to spatter paint over the surface. (Photo 2) *Option:* Pull the palette knife across the bristles instead of your thumb.

**Photo 1.** Loading a toothbrush with thinned paint.

**Photo 2.** Flyspecking the surface.

## PAINTING TIPS

• When loading a brush with a different color, but one that is in the same color family, it is preferable to wipe the brush on a damp paper towel to remove excess paint before loading a new color. Avoid rinsing the brush too often in water.

• When loading your brush with a color in a different color family, the brush does not need to be thoroughly cleaned. Simply rinse in water and blot brush on a paper towel to remove excess water. Then load the brush with a new color.

• Sometimes I paint with a "dirty brush." Leaving some of the color in the brush from another element seems to blend the colors together better. For example, if I want to add a reddish tint to a leaf, I will leave a little green in my brush when I load the red so that the colors can "marry."

# Finishing Your Piece

A clear varnish or sealer is needed to protect the painted surface. For wood surfaces, I apply two or more coats of **waterbase varnish** as follows:

1. Let the painting thoroughly dry and cure. Using a **synthetic bristle brush or sponge brush**, apply a coat of brush-on varnish. Let dry.
2. Rub the surface with a piece of a brown paper bag with no printing on it to smooth the surface.
3. Apply a final coat of varnish or a coat of clear **paste wax**.

For some projects, a spray finish may be preferable. The recommended finish is included in the individual instructions for each project.

# PAINTING ON WOOD

Wood is a wonderful surface for painting, and in
this section you'll see an array of techniques for
enhancing wood surfaces with paint. You can use these
techniques on accessories or furniture pieces,
on new wood or old.

# Preparing New Wood

Generally, I don't seal raw wood before basecoating with acrylic paint because paint adheres better to unsealed wood. However, if there are knotholes or the wood is green, I apply a light coat of matte acrylic varnish to seal the flaws before applying paint.

**Here's how to prepare a new piece for painting:**
1. Sand piece with medium, then fine grade sandpaper. Wipe with a tack cloth.
2. Apply a light coat of varnish to seal any knotholes or green wood. Let dry.
3. If the sealer has raised the grain of the wood, sand lightly with fine sandpaper and wipe with a tack cloth.

# Preparing Old Wood

If the paint on an old piece is in good condition, cleaning the piece with soap and water and allowing it to dry completely may be all that's needed. To remove dirt, dust, cobwebs, or grease, use a cleaner that does not leave a gritty residue. Effective cleaners include **mild dishwashing detergent** and **bubble bath**. Mix the cleaner with water and wash the furniture with a cellulose sponge. Rinse and wipe dry with soft cloth rags. Let dry completely.

If the paint is chipped or flaking, but you want to keep the paint color and the old, distressed look, you will need to clean the piece and remove some of the chipped paint so your new painting won't flake away.
1. Sand away any loose paint.
2. Wipe with a tack cloth.
3. Wipe with a liquid sanding preparation. Let dry thoroughly.
4. Transfer the design and proceed with painting.

# Basecoating

The basecoat is the paint you apply to the surface before the design is transferred. If the paint on an old piece cannot be rescued or you don't like the color or if your piece is new, a fresh basecoat is necessary. Before you start, be sure the paint you apply is compatible with the type of paint you will use to do the decorative painting. If you are not sure, take a sample of your paint to a good paint store and ask them what type of paint you need.

**Here's how to apply a new basecoat on an old piece:**
1. Clean the surface.
2. Using medium grade sandpaper, sand the surface thoroughly.
3. Wipe with a tack cloth.
4. Apply a coat of stain blocker or gesso. Allow to dry thoroughly and sand again. Wipe with a tack cloth.
5. Apply several coats of paint in your desired color, sanding between coats.

**Here's how to basecoat a new piece:**
1. With a small roller, a sponge brush, or a synthetic bristle brush, apply a generous amount of paint. Let dry.
2. Rub with a piece of a brown paper bag with no printing on it to smooth the painted wood.
3. Apply a second coat of the base color if needed for complete coverage. Let dry.
4. Use a piece of a brown paper bag to smooth the surface again. Sometimes a third coat of paint is necessary for full coverage.

# Summer Ferns
## m e m o r y   b o x

This large box is great for storing photographs, keepsakes, the family bible, or mementos. The project is easier than it may appear. Crumpled plastic wrap was pressed over paint to create the textured background, the fern motifs were painted using stamps, and the monogram was done with ink pens.

### TECHNIQUES TO LEARN:

Texturing a background
Stamping a design
Inking a design

### STAMPING TIPS

• Practice stamping on paper before stamping on your project.

• Don't use too much paint.

• Blot the loaded stamp on a paper towel or palette before you stamp on the box.

• Don't be afraid to stamp a second time.

• Clean the stamp(s) after each color combination and dry on a rag or towel.

# Summer Ferns
## memory box

*Pictured on page 28*

## SUPPLIES

**Artist Pigment Acrylic Paints:**
Green Dark
Green Light
Green Medium
True Burgundy
Warm White
Yellow Citron

**Acrylic Craft Paints:**
Licorice
Linen
Solid Bronze (metallic)

**Brushes:**
Flats - #4, #10
Liner - #1
Round - #4

**Surface:**
Long oval wooden box, 12" x 20"

**Other Supplies:**
*In addition to the Basic Painting Supplies listed on page 14, you'll need:*
Glazing medium
Blending medium
Sponge brushes for basecoating
Toothpick, round sponge-on-a-stick applicator, pencil with a new eraser, or stylus for making tiny berries
Clear tape
Plastic wrap for creating textured background
Foam Stamp - Fern motif, your choice
*Option:* Leaf motif
Black permanent ink markers in various sizes for inking
Clear acrylic spray sealer
Paper to practice stamping
Waterbase varnish

## PALETTE OF COLORS

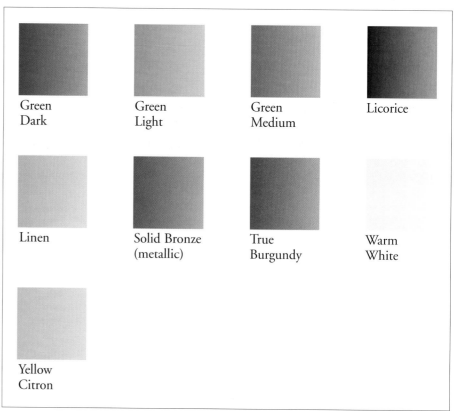

Green Dark

Green Light

Green Medium

Licorice

Linen

Solid Bronze (metallic)

True Burgundy

Warm White

Yellow Citron

## INSTRUCTIONS

**Prepare the Surface:**
1. Sand the box (if necessary) and wipe with a tack cloth.
2. Use a good wood filler (if needed) to fill any holes, then sand lightly and wipe with tack rag.
3. Using a sponge brush, paint the base of the box with Licorice. It probably will take two coats to cover. Let dry.
4. Rub with a piece of brown paper bag with no printing on it to smooth the surface.
5. Using a sponge brush, paint the lid of the box with three coats Warm White. Let dry.
6. Rub with a piece of brown paper bag with no printing on it to smooth the surface.
7. Squeeze two parts glazing medium and one part Linen on a palette. (Here, I'm using a piece of glass—Photo 1). Mix with a palette knife (Photo 2). Brush over the lid (Photo 3).
8. Quickly crumple a piece of plastic wrap in your hand and press it over the wet glazing medium mix, creating texture (Photo 4). Remove plastic. Let dry.
9. Tape off the border and paint with two coats Licorice. (Figs. 1 and 2 on worksheet)

10. Using your liner brush, trim the edges of the border with Solid Bronze. (Fig. 2)
11. Neatly trace the vine and leaf pattern. Transfer with white transfer paper or chalk on the border. (Fig. 3)

## Stamp the Ferns:

1. Fill your #1 liner brush with Yellow Citron that has been thinned with water to a very thin flowing consistency. Neatly paint the vines (Photo 5, Fig. 3).
2. Brush the stamp with blending medium (Photo 6).
3. Load the paint (color mixes are listed below) onto the fern stamp, using a small paint brush (Photo 7).
4. Stamp the design onto the box (Photo 8, Fig. 4), using the photo and the pattern as guides for placement. *Practice stamping first on a piece of paper before stamping on the box.* Let box dry.
5. If additional shading is desired, carefully wash the colors of your choice on the leaves here and there. See the worksheets for examples.

## Color Mixes for Ferns and Leaves:

Most any combination you wish to try will work. See the Stamped Ferns Worksheet for examples.
• Yellow Citron on one side, Green Medium on the other side
• Yellow Citron on one side, Green Dark on the other side
• Green Medium on one side, Green Dark on the other side
• Green Dark          • Green Medium
*Options:* Add some Solid Bronze to any color combination. Add veins and details with Green Dark, Green Dark + True Burgundy, or Yellow Citron.

## Paint the Berries:

*Some are small, some large.*

1. Apply the small dots representing berries with Solid Bronze and Warm White, using the handle of your paint brush, a stylus, a toothpick, or a round sponge-on-a-stick applicator. You could use the eraser of a pencil to make larger dots (Photo 9, Fig. 4).

*continued on next page*

**Photo 1.** Squeezing paint to mix with glazing medium.

**Photo 2.** Mixing paint and glazing medium with a palette knife.

**Photo 3.** Brushing the glazing mix on the surface with sponge brush.

**Photo 4.** Pressing crumpled plastic wrap over the wet surface to create texture.

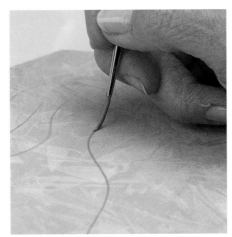

**Photo 5.** Painting the vines.

**Photo 6.** Applying blending medium to a stamp.

**Photo 7.** Loading the stamp with paint, using a brush.

**Photo 8.** Pressing the stamp on the surface.

**Photo 9.** Adding dots for berries with brush handle.

*Continued from page 31*

2. Paint the stems using a #1 liner brush full of thinned Green Medium.
3. Highlight the stems with a little Green Light. Let dry and cure.

**Ink the Center Design:**

1. Neatly trace and transfer the design.

2. Carefully fill in the lines using various sizes of permanent ink pens.

**Finish:**

1. When the paint is thoroughly cured, mist lightly with a clear acrylic spray to keep the ink from bleeding.
2. Varnish with three or four coats of waterbase varnish. ❏

# Stamped Ferns Worksheet

Fig. 1 - Paint band with Licorice.

Fig. 2 - Apply a second coat of Licorice. Outline band with Solid bronze.

Fig. 3 - Transfer vine pattern to band. Paint vines with Yellow Citron.

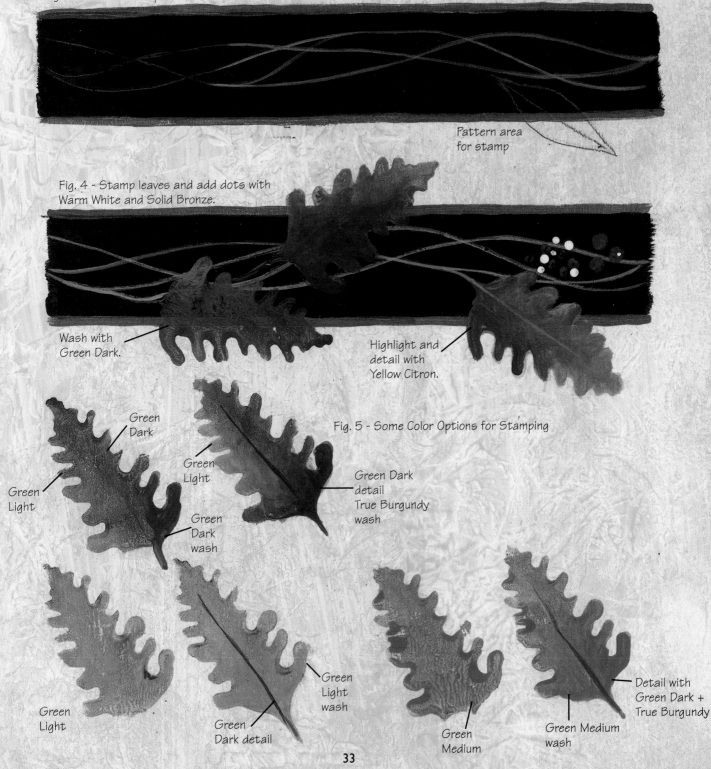

Pattern area for stamp

Fig. 4 - Stamp leaves and add dots with Warm White and Solid Bronze.

Wash with Green Dark.

Highlight and detail with Yellow Citron.

Green Dark

Green Light

Green Light

Green Dark wash

Fig. 5 - Some Color Options for Stamping

Green Dark detail True Burgundy wash

Green Light wash

Green Light

Green Dark detail

Green Medium

Green Medium wash

Detail with Green Dark + True Burgundy

# Pattern for Summer Ferns Memory Box

(Enlarge @200% for actual size.)

*Instructions begin on page 30.*

Pattern for In Full Bloom
Framed Mirror

(actual size)

*Instructions begin on page 38.*

# In Full Bloom
## framed mirror

Mirror, mirror on the wall, who is the fairest one of all? This charming mirror will add a unique touch in almost any room of your home. Yes, it could be used as a picture frame. But after all, a mirror is a picture of a multitude of faces.

I have chosen to adorn this mirror frame with roses, and in the pages that follow, you'll learn how to paint beautiful roses, step by step.

### TECHNIQUES TO LEARN:

Stenciling with a texture medium

Painting roses

*Instructions begin on page 38*

# In Full Bloom
## framed mirror

*Pictured on page 34-35*

## SUPPLIES

**Artist Pigment Acrylic Paints:**

Asphaltum

Burnt Sienna

Green Light

Green Medium

Green Umber

Ice Green

True Burgundy

Titanium White

**Acrylic Craft Paints:**

Buttercup

Copper (metallic)

**Brushes:**

Flats - #8, #10

Liner - #1

Wash Brush - 1"

**Surface:**

Mirror with flat, wide wooden frame

**Other Supplies:**

*In addition to the Basic Painting Supplies listed on page 14, you'll need:*

Stencil with vine and leaf border motifs

Blending medium

Glazing medium

Clear tape

Modeling paste texture medium

*Pattern appears on page 35.*

## PALETTE OF COLORS

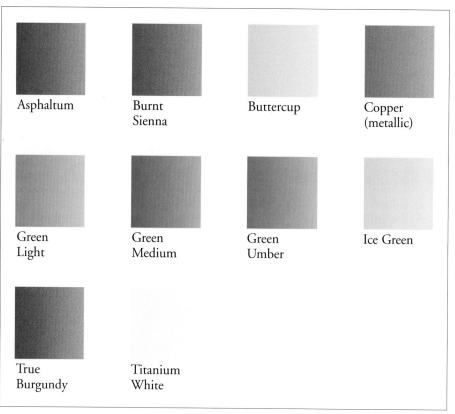

Asphaltum

Burnt Sienna

Buttercup

Copper (metallic)

Green Light

Green Medium

Green Umber

Ice Green

True Burgundy

Titanium White

## INSTRUCTIONS

**Prepare the Surface:**

1. Sand the mirror frame and wipe with a tack cloth.
2. Apply two or three coats Buttercup. Let the paint dry between coats.
3. Rub with piece of brown bag with no printing on it to smooth the nap of the wood.
4. Position the border stencil, using the photo as a guide. Apply modeling paste with a palette knife through the stencil openings. Lift the stencil. Re-position and repeat in the opposite corner. Let the paste dry. See the Leaf Worksheet that follows these instructions for an example.
5. Neatly trace and transfer the design.
6. Double load your #1 wash brush with glazing medium and Asphaltum. *Option:* Add a touch of Burnt Sienna to the Asphaltum to redden the color.
7. Pat or stroke this color around the outside edge of the design, placing the dark next to the design and fading out the color into the background. Let dry.

**Paint the Leaves:**

*See the Leaf Worksheet that follows these instructions.*

1. Undercoat the leaves with two coats Green Medium. Let the paint dry between coats. (Fig. 1)

2. Double load your flat brush with blending gel or water and Green Umber. Blend on the palette to soften the color. Float Green Umber shadows at the bases of the leaves. (Fig. 2) Let dry.

3. Apply a thin coat of blending medium to the dried leaf, then the colors of your choice. On the worksheet, I applied more Green Umber at the base, then Green Medium and Green Light and, at the top, Ice Green. (Fig. 3)

4. Quickly wipe your brush. Using an extremely light touch, blend from the base of the leaf out to the edge. (Fig. 4)

5. Accent the outside edges of the leaf with strokes of Green Light and Ice Green, stroking from the outside edge back towards the base. (Figs. 5 and 6)

### Paint the Roses:

*See the "Painting a Rose" photo sequence. Also see the Rose Worksheet that follows these instructions. Figure numbers reference the worksheet.*

1. Make a dark mixture of True Burgundy + Burnt Sienna (1:1). Make a light mixture of this dark mix + Titanium White (1:3).

2. Neatly undercoat the roses with the dark mix. Let dry. Apply a second coat. (Photos 1 and 2, Fig. 1) Let dry.

3. Working one rose at a time, apply a little blending medium to the entire rose. Double load a flat brush with the light mixture and dark mixture. Be sure the brush is full of paint that is a flowing consistency.

4. Paint strokes all the way around the outside edge of the rose. (Photo 3, Fig. 2)

5. Paint a second row of petals. (Photo 4, Fig. 3)

6. Paint a third row of petals. (Fig. 4)

7. Paint the bowl of the rose, connecting to the inner edges of the third row of petals. (Fig. 4)

8. Paint the bottom of the bowl. (Photo 5)

9. Add comma-like strokes to fill the empty spaces. (Fig. 5, Photo 6) Let your paint dry.

### Finish:

1. Using tape, mask off a border around the mirror opening. Paint the border with two coats Copper. Let dry. Remove tape.

2. Double load the #1 wash brush with Asphaltum and glazing medium. Shade around the outer edge of the mirror border, the stenciled motifs, and the outer edge of the mirror frame. Let dry.

3. Trim the outside edge of the frame with Copper. Let dry.

4. Varnish with two or more coats of waterbase varnish. ❑

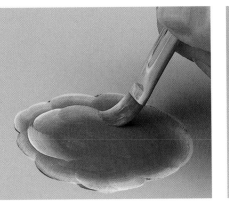

**Photo 1.** Undercoating the outer petals.

**Photo 2.** Undercoating the inner petals.

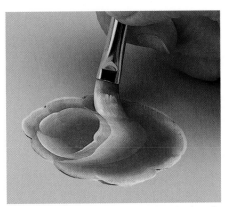

**Photo 3.** Stroking the outer petals with the light and dark mix.

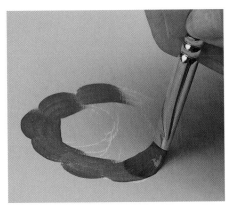

**Photo 4.** Stroking the inner petals.

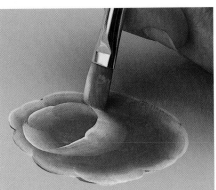

**Photo 5.** Stroking the bowl.

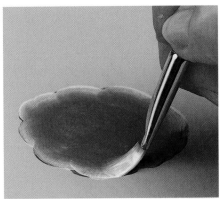

**Photo 6.** Adding strokes under the bowl.

# Leaf Worksheet

The Stenciled Border:

Apply modeling paste through the openings of a stencil. Let dry. Float Asphaltum, using a 1" wash brush to shade around the design.

Fig. 1 - Undercoat with Green Medium.

Fig. 2 - Float Green Umber at base. Let dry.

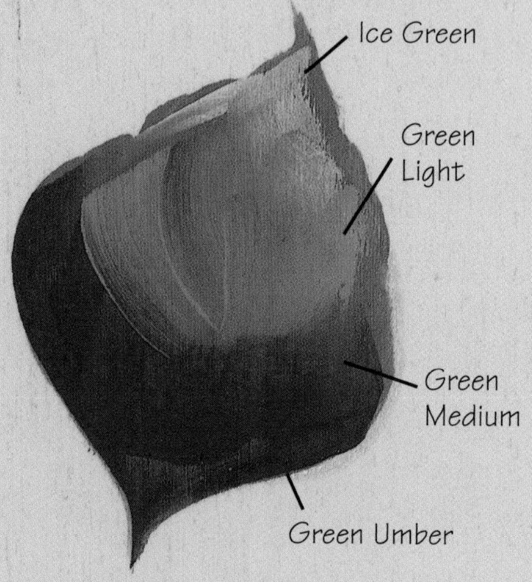

Ice Green

Green Light

Green Medium

Green Umber

Fig. 3 - Apply blending medium and colors.

Fig. 4 - Blend, using a light touch.

Fig. 5 - Accent with strokes of Green Light and Ice Green.

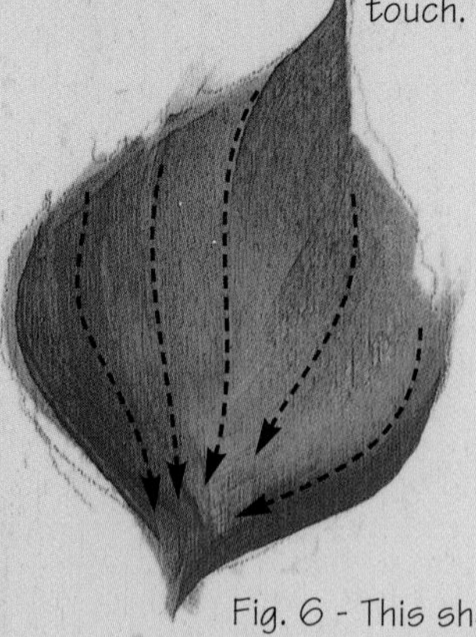

Fig. 6 - This shows the blending direction for the accent strokes.

Hauser

# Rose Worksheet

Dark
Mix

Light
Mix

Fig. 1 - Neatly undercoat with dark mix. Apply a second coat if needed. Let dry. Apply blending medium.

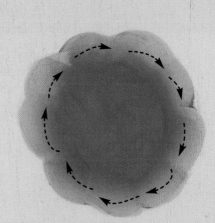

Fig. 2 - Double load a flat brush with dark mix and light mix. Paint outer petals.

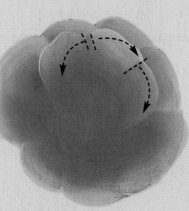

Fig. 3 - Paint second row of petals.

Fig. 4 - Paint third row, then paint the bowl.

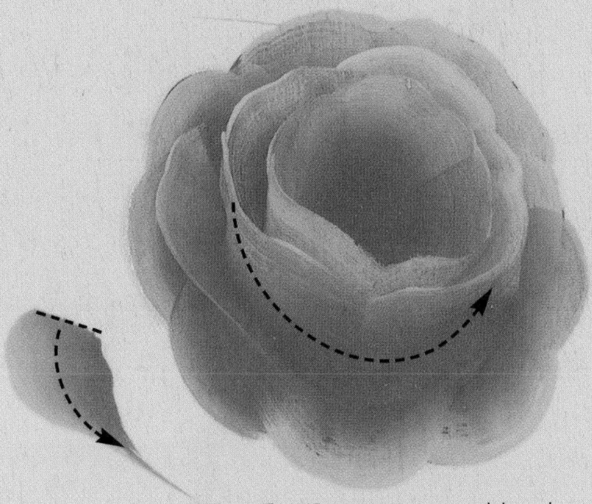

Fig. 5 - Paint a second bowl around the first. Fill with comma strokes.

Fig. 6 -
A finished rose.

# Basket of Daisies
## wooden photo album

Daisies are such happy flowers, and I love the way they look gathered in a basket. The painted background of the album was flyspecked before the design was painted. The basket is stenciled and given dimension with modeling paste, applied through the openings of the stencil. Additional dimension is provided with shading and shadowing.

Daisies are easy to paint if you know brush strokes. Complete instructions for painting daisies appear with the Daisy Bouquet Watering Can project.

### TECHNIQUES TO LEARN:

Stenciling with a texture medium
Flyspecking
Painting brush stroke daisies

*Instructions begin on page 44.*

# Basket of Daisies
## w o o d e n   a l b u m

*Pictured on page 42-43*

## SUPPLIES

**Artist Pigment Acrylic Paints:**

Asphaltum

Burnt Sienna

Burnt Umber

Green Dark

Green Light

Green Medium

Green Umber

Medium Yellow

Payne's Gray

Titanium White

Warm White

**Acrylic Craft Paints:**

Autumn Leaves

Wicker White

**Brushes:**

Flats - #4, #6, #10, #12

Liner - Liner #1

Glaze/wash - 1"

**Surface:**

Wooden photo album cover, 12" x 12"

**Other Supplies:**

*In addition to the Basic Painting Supplies listed on page 14, you'll need:*

Modeling paste texture medium

Stencil blank material

Good scissors *or* a craft knife *or* hot tool stencil cutter for cutting the stencil design

Toothbrush for flyspecking

Sponge brush for basecoating surface

## PALETTE OF COLORS

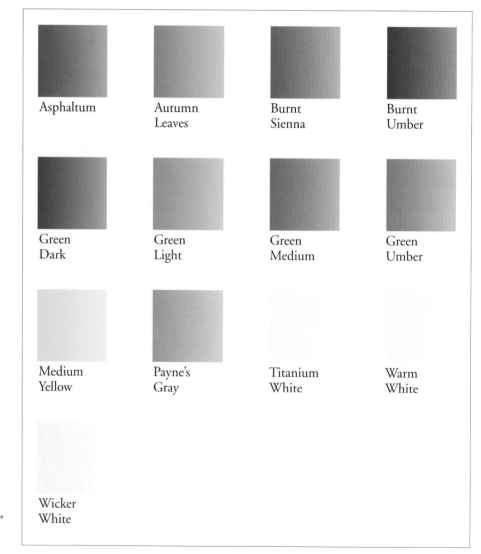

Asphaltum

Autumn Leaves

Burnt Sienna

Burnt Umber

Green Dark

Green Light

Green Medium

Green Umber

Medium Yellow

Payne's Gray

Titanium White

Warm White

Wicker White

## INSTRUCTIONS

**Prepare the Surface:**

1. Remove the hardware from the album and set aside. Sand the surface. Wipe with a tack cloth.
2. Mix three parts Autumn Leaves + one part Wicker White (3:1).
3. Using a sponge brush, apply two coats of the mix to the front and back. Let paint dry thoroughly between coats.
4. Rub with a piece of brown paper bag with no printing on it to smooth the nap of the wood.

*Continued on page 46*

**Photo 1.** Loading a toothbrush with thinned Wicker White.

**Photo 2.** Flyspecking the surface.

**Photo 3.** Cutting the stencil with stencil cutter tool.

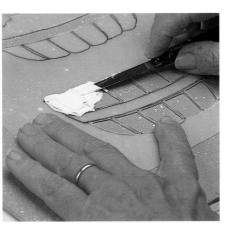

**Photo 4.** Applying modeling paste.

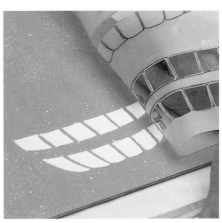

**Photo 5.** Lifting the stencil.

**Photo 6.** Painting the basket slats.

**Photo 7.** Using a cloth to rub out highlights.

*continued from page 44*

5. Load a toothbrush with thinned Wicker White (Photo 1) and flyspeck the album, pulling your thumb over the bristles so that flecks of paint fall on the surface (Photo 2), both front and back. Let dry thoroughly.

6. Double load the 1" wash brush with Asphaltum on one side and blending medium on the other. Blend on the palette so the color graduates through the hairs of the brush from dark to medium to light.

7. Shade all the way around the front edge of the scrapbook. Let dry. Repeat on the back.

8. Paint the inside with Autumn Leaves. Let dry.

9. Neatly trace and transfer the pattern using gray or white graphite paper.

**Stencil the Basket:**

*This is a two-part stencil.*

1. Trace the pattern on stencil blank material.

2. Cut out the stencil. If cutting with a craft knife, work on a piece of glass. If cutting with scissors, cut neatly and carefully. I like to use a hot tool such as a stencil cutter. (Photo 3)

3. Position the first overlay on the album. Secure with a piece of tape.

4. Using a straight blade palette knife, apply modeling paste to the surface through the stencil openings. (Photo 4) Carefully remove the stencil. (Photo 5) Let dry.

5. Position the second overlay. (This is the band that goes across the basket.) Apply the modeling paste. Carefully lift the stencil. Let dry thoroughly.

6. Apply a bit of blending medium to the slats, then Burnt Umber. (Photo 6) Use a soft cloth to wipe out the centers, creating highlights. (Photo 7)

7. *Option:* Shade the edges darker with Burnt Umber. (This is something you will want to play with a little bit. No two baskets turn out the same, but they are all delightful.)

8. Trace and transfer the daisy design.

**Paint the Leaves:**

1. Paint the leaves, following the instructions and worksheet examples for the leaves in the Bird's Nest & Eggs Coat Rack project.

2. Add veins with Green Dark.

**Paint the Daisies:**

Paint the daisies, following the instructions and worksheet examples for the Daisy Bouquet Watering Can project.

**Paint the Shadow:**

1. To create the shadow under the basket, double load a large flat brush with Burnt Umber and/or a touch of Asphaltum on one side and blending medium on the other. Blend on the palette to soften the color.

2. Paint a comma-like stroke with the darkest part next to the basket. (You want it to shade from the dark to the medium to the light.) Let dry.

**Finish:**

Varnish with two or more coats of waterbase varnish. ❏

Patterns for Stencils

(Enlarge @165% for actual size)

Part 1

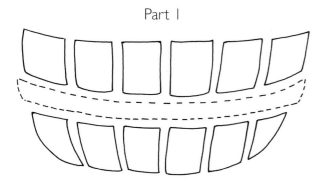

Part 2

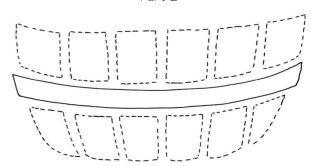

Pattern for Basket of Daisies Album Cover

(actual size)

# Bird's Nest & Eggs
## coat rack

I get so excited in the spring when the birds build their nests and lay eggs. I won't go near them (or let anyone else go near them, either.) How exciting it is when those eggs hatch and the baby birds make their way into the world! There is nothing more wonderful than watching a mother bird care for her little ones. This versatile design can be modified to accommodate a variety of surfaces—try it on the wooden coat rack (as I did here), on a cupboard door or the drawer fronts of a dresser, or on a paper lampshade. The leafy vines would make a wonderful border for a chair back or picture frame.

### TECHNIQUES TO LEARN:

Painting on raw wood
Painting a nest and eggs
Linework details

*Instructions begin on page 50.*

48

# Bird's Nest & Eggs
## coat rack

*Pictured on page 48-49*

## SUPPLIES

**Artist Pigment Acrylic Paints:**

Burnt Umber

Green Light

Green Medium

Green Umber

Payne's Gray

Raw Sienna

Warm White

Yellow Ochre

**Brushes:**

Flats - #4, #8, #10, #14

Liner - #1

Filbert - #6

**Surface:**

Wooden coat rack with pegs,
   approx. 19" wide

**Other Supplies:**

*In addition to the Basic Painting Supplies
   listed on page 14, you'll need:*

Blending medium

*Pattern appears on page 54.*

## PALETTE OF COLORS

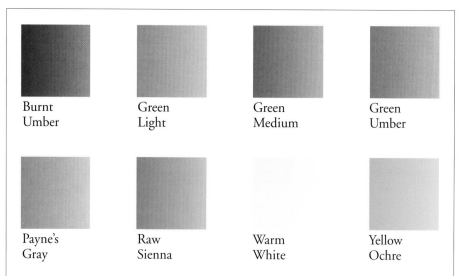

Burnt Umber

Green Light

Green Medium

Green Umber

Payne's Gray

Raw Sienna

Warm White

Yellow Ochre

## INSTRUCTIONS

**Prepare the Surface:**

*This design is painted on the raw wood.*

1. Sand the rack and wipe with the tack cloth.

2. Neatly trace and transfer the design, using a light touch. You don't want those lines to be too heavy. (Photos 1 & 2)

**Paint the Leaves:**

*All leaves are painted the same way. Paint the leaf underneath the nest first. Then paint the stems and vines, then the other leaves. See the Bird's Nest Worksheet.*

*Continued on page 52*

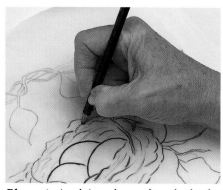

**Photo 1.** Applying charcoal to the back of the traced design.

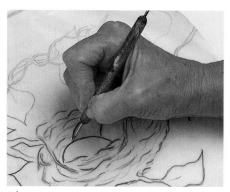

**Photo 2.** Using a stylus to transfer.

# Bird's Nest Worksheet

Fig. 1 - Apply blending medium to entire leaf. Stroke on Green Umber.

Fig. 2 - Blend in Green Medium and Green Light.

Fig. 3 - Blend in Warm White at tip.

Fig. 4 - Add vein with thinned Burnt Umber. Highlight with Yellow Ochre + Warm White (1:1).

Fig. 5 - Undercoat nest with Yellow Ochre + Warm White (1:1). *The photos show undercoating with Burnt Umber. This is an alternative. Either color will be fine for undercoating. Undercoat eggs with Warm White + touches of Payne's Gray + Burnt Umber.*

Fig. 6 - Apply blending medium to nest. Shade with Burnt Umber. Apply blending medium to eggs and shade with Payne's Gray.

Fig. 7 - Using a liner brush with Yellow Ochre + Warm White (1:1), paint lines on nest.
Using the tip of a #6 filbert, dab a Payne's Gray wash on eggs.

Fig. 8 - Paint Burnt Umber lines on nest. Highlight lines with Yellow Ochre + Warm White (1:4).
Dab Warm White highlights on eggs.

Fig. 9 - Paint branches with a Burnt Umber wash.

Fig. 10 - Add Burnt Umber lines to bottom third of branches.

Fig. 11 - Paint vines with Yellow Ochre + Warm White (1:1). Shade with Burnt Umber. Highlight with Yellow Ochre + Warm White (1:4).

*continued from page 50*

1. Apply a small amount of blending medium to the entire leaf. (Fig. 1)
2. Float Green Umber on the base of the leaf. (Fig. 1)
3. Apply a little Green Medium and Green Light. Blend the two colors together. (Fig. 2)
4. Add a touch of Warm White to the tip of the leaf and blend. (Fig. 3)
5. To create the vein, fill a liner brush with thinned Burnt Umber and carefully paint a thin vein. Highlight with Yellow Ochre + Warm White (1:1). (Fig. 4)

## Paint the Branches:
*See the Bird's Nest Worksheet, Figs. 9 and 10.*
1. Using a small flat brush, paint the branches with thinned Burnt Umber. *TIP:* Thin the Burnt Umber with blending medium. Be careful about using water—it can cause the paint to bleed on the raw wood.
2. Fill your liner brush with thinned Burnt Umber. Paint Burnt Umber lines along the bottom third of the branches.

## Paint the Vines:
*See the Bird's Nest Worksheet, Fig. 11.*
1. Use the small flat brush loaded with a mixture of Yellow Ochre + Warm White (1:1) to pull the vines so that they intertwine with the branch and the leaves.
2. Shade with thinned Burnt Umber.
3. Highlight with a mixture of Yellow Ochre + Warm White (1:4). TIP: Use a touch of blending medium to help you with your blending, as it will keep the paint wet.

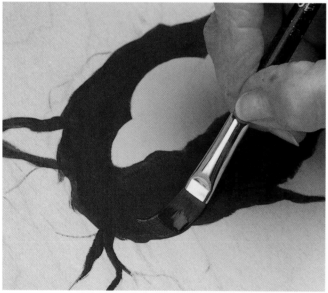

**Photo 3.** Undercoating the nest.

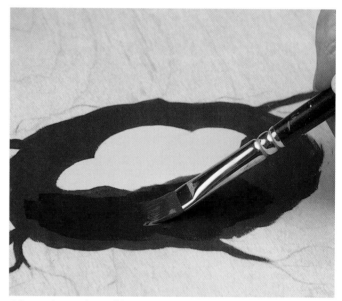

**Photo 4.** Applying blending medium to the nest.

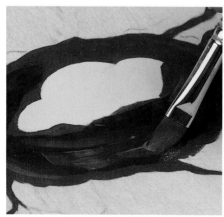

**Photo 5.** Applying shading of Raw Sienna to the nest.

**Photo 6.** Double loading the brush with blending medium and Payne's Gray for shading the eggs.

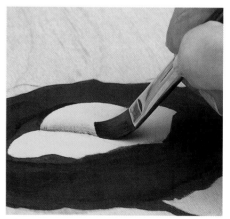

**Photo 7.** Shading the eggs with Payne's Gray.

**Paint the Nest & Eggs:**

1. Undercoat the eggs with a mixture of Warm White + tiny touches Payne's Gray + Burnt Umber. (Fig. 5) Let dry.
2. Neatly undercoat the nest with Burnt Umber. (Photo 3 and Fig. 5)
3. Apply blending medium to the entire nest. (Photo 4)
4. Double load your brush with blending medium and Raw Sienna and shade around the eggs and across the front of the nest. (Photo 5 and Fig. 6)
5. Apply blending medium to the eggs. Shade with a double loaded brush of blending medium and Payne's Gray. (Photo 7)
6. Mix a wash with a touch of Payne's Gray and water so it is very thin. Blend on the eggs. (Photo 8.)

*continued on page 54*

**Photo 8.** Applying a wash of Payne's Gray to the eggs.

**Photo 9.** Dabbing the Payne's Gray wash on the eggs for a mottled look.

**Photo 10.** Using a flat brush to add lines of Yellow Ochre + Warm White for more nest material(1:1).

**Photo 11.** Adding more lines of Yellow Ochre + Warm White (1:4).

**Photo 12.** Using the Yellow Ochre + Warm White (1:4) mix to pull some straw across the nest with the liner.

**Photo 13.** Highlighting the nest material.

*continued from page 53*

7. Use a #6 filbert brush to dab eggs with the Payne's Gray wash for a mottled look. (Photo 9 and Fig. 7) Let dry.

8. Highlight the tops of the eggs using a brush double loaded with blending medium and Warm White. (Fig. 8)

9. Pull some lines across the top of the nest also using Yellow Ochre + Warm White. (Photo 10)

10. Build the nest by adding more lines with Burnt Umber. Highlight with Warm White. Add additional lines of Yellow Ochre + Warm White if needed. (Photo 11) Let dry.

11. To finish the nest, fill your liner brush with a mixture of Yellow Ochre + Warm White (1:1). Paint fine lines over the nest. (Photo 12 and Fig. 7) TIP: Remember, when I say liner, you say thin. Thin the paint with water so that it will flow from the point of the liner brush as ink would flow from a fountain pen.

**Finish:**

1. Varnish with two coats waterbase varnish. Let dry.

2. Rub with a piece of brown paper bag with no printing on it to smooth the nap of the wood.

3. Apply a final coat of varnish. ❏

## Pattern for Bird's Nest & Eggs Coat Rack
### (actual size)

Part A

Connect Part A to Part B
at dotted lines to complete
the pattern.

Part B

# Bird in a Frame
## framed painting

Birds are delicate, dainty creatures that can be painted in an array of magnificent colors. The background of this shadow box frame was designed to enhance the bird's coloring. Sponged metallic paint was added over the background color to create a shimmering, textured background.

### TECHNIQUES TO LEARN:
Metallic sponging on background
Painting on black
Painting a bird

## SUPPLIES

**Artist Pigment Acrylic Paints:**
Asphaltum
Green Dark
Green Light
Green Medium
Payne's Gray
Raw Sienna
Warm White

**Acrylic Craft Paints:**
Bayberry
Inca Gold (metallic)
Licorice
Portrait Light

**Brushes:**
Flats - #4, #8
Liners - #1, #2-0

**Surface:**
Wooden shadow box frame,
    size 8" x 8" x 1-1/2"
Wooden oval plaque, size 3-1/2" x 5"

**Other Supplies:**
*In addition to the Basic Painting Supplies listed on page 14, you'll need:*
Blending medium
Glazing medium
Small dauber tool, 1/4" diameter
Sponge brush for basecoating
Natural sea sponge
Small block of wood, 1/4" thick,
    1" square
Glue, wood glue or all-purpose

## PALETTE OF COLORS

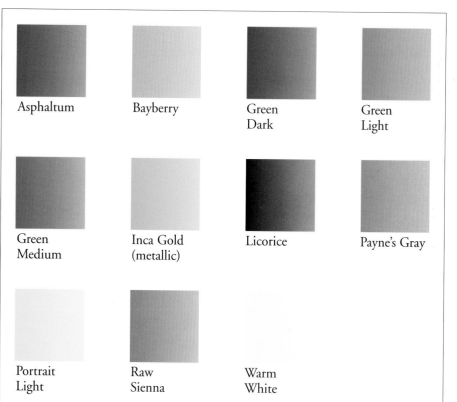

Asphaltum

Bayberry

Green Dark

Green Light

Green Medium

Inca Gold (metallic)

Licorice

Payne's Gray

Portrait Light

Raw Sienna

Warm White

## INSTRUCTIONS

**Prepare the Surfaces:**
1. Sand the oval and the frame. Wipe with a tack cloth.
2. Paint the inside of the frame with two coats Bayberry, using the 1" sponge brush.
3. Paint the outside portion of the frame with two coats Licorice. Let dry.
4. Rub with a piece of brown paper bag with no printing on it to smooth the nap of the wood.
5. Dampen the sea sponge. Dip the sponge in glazing medium and pounce over the Bayberry area of the frame. (Photo 1). Don't rinse the sponge.
6. Pour a puddle of Inca Gold on your palette. Pounce the sponge in the Inca Gold. (Photo 2) Blot on a paper towel. (Photo 3)

*Continued on page 58*

*continued from page 56*

7. Lightly dab the gold over the Bayberry surface. (Photo 4) Let dry. If you get gold on the black part of the frame, touch up with Licorice.

8. Paint the oval with two coats of Licorice. Let the paint dry between coats.

9. Rub with a piece of brown paper bag with no printing on it to smooth the nap of the wood.

10. Using your small flat brush, trim the edge of the oval with two coats of Warm White.

11. Neatly trace and transfer the design to the oval, using white transfer paper or chalk.

**Paint the Bird:**

*See the Bird Worksheet and the step-by-step photos.*

1. Carefully undercoat the bird with two coats of Bayberry. (Fig. 1, Photo 5) Let the paint dry between coats.

2. Pick up Green Medium with the small dauber and blot on a rag. Dab Green Medium across the top of the head, down the back, and on the tail. (Fig. 2)

3. Dab breast with Warm White + Bayberry. (Fig. 2)

4. Pick up Green Dark on the dauber and darken the top of the head, the back, and the tail. (Fig. 3, Photo 6)

5. Pick up Portrait Light on the dauber and dab on the breast and the underside of the tail.

6. Outline the tail feathers with Green Light.

**Photo 1.** Pouncing the frame with glazing medium.

**Photo 2.** Pouncing the sponge in Inca Gold.

**Photo 3.** Blotting the sponge on a paper towel.

**Photo 4.** Dabbing the surface with Inca Gold.

58

7. Stroke the dark tail feathers with Payne's Gray + Warm White (1:1). (Fig. 3)

8. Pick up Warm White and dab on the breast area and the eye area. (Fig. 3, Photo 7)

9. Paint the eye and the beak with Payne's Gray.

10. Highlight the beak with a touch of Warm White so it stands out against the black background. (Fig. 4)

11. Highlight the eye with Warm White. (Fig. 4)

12. If needed, neatly outline the tail with a tiny touch of Green Light.

13. Load a flat brush with blending medium. Pick up Warm White on the edge. Carefully stroke the breast feathers. (Photo 8, Fig. 4)

Continued on page 61

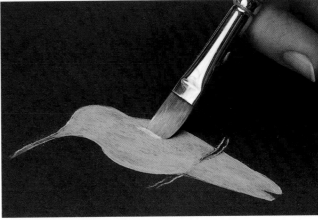

**Photo 5.** Undercoating with Bayberry.

**Photo 6.** Darkening with Green Dark, using a dauber.

**Photo 7.** Dabbing with Warm White.

**Photo 8.** Stroking the breast feathers.

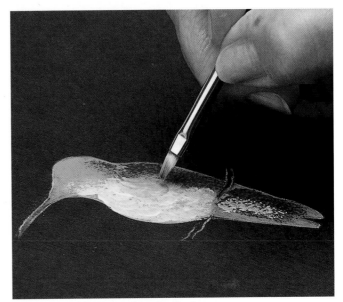

**Photo 9.** Adding detail to the feathers.

# Bird Worksheet

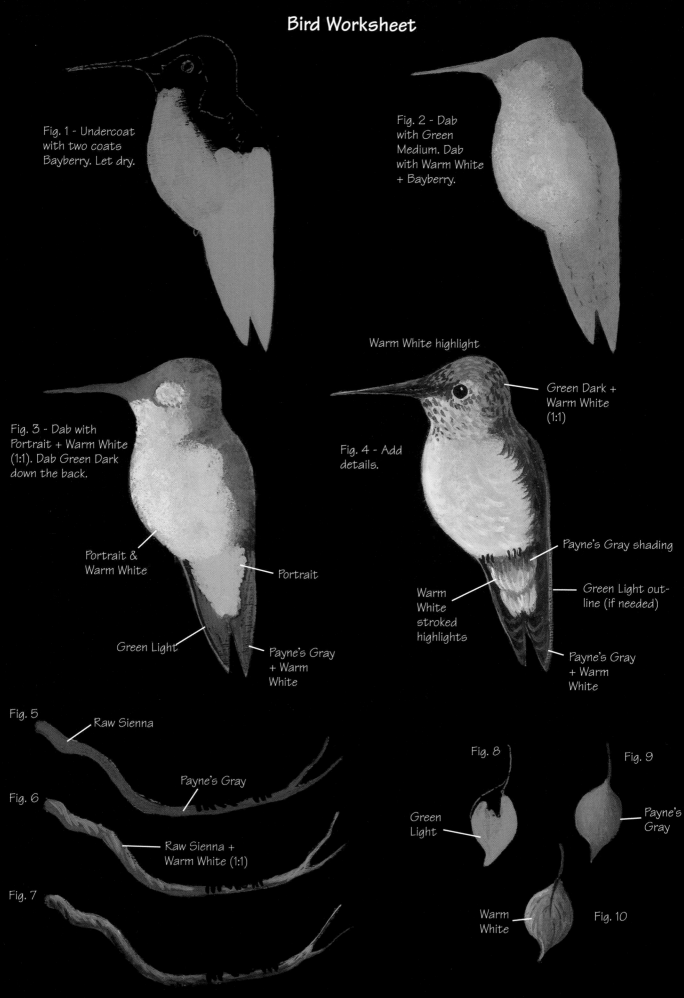

Fig. 1 - Undercoat with two coats Bayberry. Let dry.

Fig. 2 - Dab with Green Medium. Dab with Warm White + Bayberry.

Warm White highlight

Fig. 3 - Dab with Portrait + Warm White (1:1). Dab Green Dark down the back.

Portrait & Warm White

Portrait

Green Light

Payne's Gray + Warm White

Fig. 4 - Add details.

Green Dark + Warm White (1:1)

Payne's Gray shading

Green Light out-line (if needed)

Warm White stroked highlights

Payne's Gray + Warm White

Fig. 5

Raw Sienna

Payne's Gray

Fig. 6

Raw Sienna + Warm White (1:1)

Fig. 7

Fig. 8

Fig. 9

Green Light

Payne's Gray

Warm White

Fig. 10

*continued from page 59*

14. Load the same flat brush again with blending medium. Pick up Portrait Light and stroke the edges of the breast. (Fig. 4, Photo 9)
15. Shade the pink tail feathers, using a small flat brush double loaded with glazing medium and Payne's Gray. (Fig. 4)
16. Using your liner brush, highlight the individual feathers with Warm White.
17. Stroke the top of the head and the edges of the breast with Green Dark + Warm White (2:1). Add dark strokes of Payne's Gray.
18. Paint the feet with Payne's Gray. Highlight with Warm White. (Fig. 4)

## Paint the Branch:
*See the Bird Worksheet.*
1. Using a small flat brush or liner brush, undercoat the branch with Raw Sienna. (Fig. 5)
2. Shade with Payne's Gray. (Fig. 5)
3. Highlight with Raw Sienna + Warm White (1:1). (Fig. 6)
4. Further highlight with tiny touches of Warm White. (Fig. 7)

## Paint the Leaves:
*See the Bird Worksheet.*
1. Using the small flat brush, undercoat the leaves with Green Light. (Fig. 8)
2. Shade with Payne's Gray. (Fig. 9)
3. Highlight with Warm White. (Fig. 10)
4. Add details with thinned Payne's Gray, using a liner brush. Let dry and cure.

## Finish:
1. Varnish with two or three coats of waterbase varnish.
2. Glue a small block of wood to the back of the oval. Glue the oval to the inside of the frame so the oval stands forward from the inside of the frame. ❏

## Pattern for Bird in a Frame Wall Piece
### (actual size)

# Moose Meeting
## w o o d e n  b o x

The moose is one of my many favorite creatures. This box would make a wonderful gift for a man. You'll have fun not only painting the moose, but also the oak leaves and acorns.

The design is painted on the raw wood without a basecoat. Blending medium is applied as a undercoat—the medium penetrates the wood and keeps the paint on the surface.

### TECHNIQUES TO LEARN:
Painting on raw wood
Blending with a medium

*Instructions begin on page 64.*

# Moose Meeting
## wooden box

*Pictured on page 62-63*

## SUPPLIES

**Artist Pigment Acrylic Paints:**

Asphaltum

Burnt Umber

Pure Orange

Sap Green

True Burgundy

Yellow Citron

Yellow Light

Yellow Ochre

**Brushes:**

Liner - #1

Shaders/Brights (flats) - #1, #2, #4

**Surface:**

Wooden box, 5" x 8"

**Other Supplies:**

*In addition to the Basic Painting Supplies listed on page 14, you'll need:*

Blending medium

Waterbase varnish - Satin

## PALETTE OF COLORS

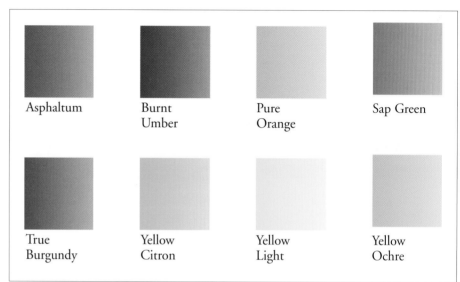

Asphaltum

Burnt Umber

Pure Orange

Sap Green

True Burgundy

Yellow Citron

Yellow Light

Yellow Ochre

## INSTRUCTIONS

**Prepare the Surface:**
1. Sand the surface, if needed, with fine grade sandpaper. Wipe with a tack cloth.
2. Neatly trace and transfer the design.

**Paint the Branches:**
*See the Moose Worksheet.*
1. Apply blending medium and let it penetrate. Apply a small amount of Yellow Ochre. (Fig. 1)
2. Keeping the branch wet with blending medium, shade with Asphaltum. Let dry slightly. (Fig. 2)
3. Reapply a little blending medium and shade with more Asphaltum. (Fig. 3)

**Paint the Vines:**
1. Mix Yellow Citron + blending medium. Paint the vine. (Fig. 4)
2. Shade with blending medium + Sap Green + a touch of Asphaltum. (Fig. 5)

**Paint the Grass:**
1. Apply blending medium, Sap Green + a tiny bit of Asphaltum. (Fig. 6)
2. Pull up blades of grass, using the chisel edge of your flat brush or your #1 liner. (Fig. 7)

*Continued on page 66*

# Moose Worksheet

Fig. 1 - Blending medium + Yellow Ochre

Fig. 2 - Blending medium + Asphaltum

Fig. 3 - Blending medium + more Asphaltum

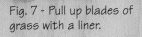

Fig. 6 - Blending medium + Sap Green + Asphaltum

Fig. 4 - Blending medium + Yellow Citron

Fig. 5 - Blending medium + Sap Green + Asphaltum

Fig. 7 - Pull up blades of grass with a liner.

Fig. 8 - Blending medium + Yellow Ochre

Fig. 9 - Blending medium + Asphaltum

Fig. 10 - Blending medium + more Asphaltum

Fig. 11 - Blending medium + Burnt Umber

Fig. 12 - Blending medium + Yellow Light

Fig. 13 - Blending medium + Pure Orange

Fig. 14 - Blending medium + True Burgundy

Fig. 15 - Blending medium + Asphaltum

Blending medium + Yellow Light

Blending medium + Pure Orange

Blending medium + True Burgundy

Blending medium + Sap Green

Fig. 16 - Blending medium + Yellow Ochre

Fig. 17 - Blending medium + Burnt Umber

*continued from page 64*

**Paint the Acorns:**

1. Apply blending medium and let it penetrate. Apply a small amount of Yellow Ochre. (Fig. 8)
2. Keep the acorns wet with blending medium and shade with a small amount of Asphaltum. (Fig. 9) Let dry slightly.
3. Apply a little more blending medium and shade a second time with Asphaltum. (Fig. 10)
4. Deepen the shadows with a tiny bit of Burnt Umber. Add more blending medium, if needed. (Fig. 11)

**Paint the Leaves:**

*This design includes two leaf shapes. They are painted the same way, but one shape has Asphaltum shading and the other shape has Sap Green shading.*

1. Apply blending medium and let it penetrate the surface. Apply Yellow Light. (Fig. 12)

2. While wet, apply Pure Orange. (Fig. 13)
3. Wipe the brush and, while the leaf is still wet, quickly shade with a small touch of True Burgundy. (Fig. 14)
4. Add just a tiny touch more blending medium. Shade with Asphaltum *or* Sap Green. (Fig. 15)

**Paint the Moose:**

1. Apply blending medium. Let it penetrate. Apply Yellow Ochre. (Fig. 16)
2. While wet, carefully apply the dark shading with Burnt Umber. Lightly blend. (Fig. 17) Let dry and cure.

**Finish:**

1. Trim the edge of the lid with Burnt Umber. Let dry thoroughly.
2. Rub the box with a piece of brown paper bag with no printing on it to smooth the nap of the wood.
3. Varnish with two or three coats of waterbase varnish. ❑

## Pattern for Moose Meeting Wooden Box
### (actual size)

Front of Box

Top of Box

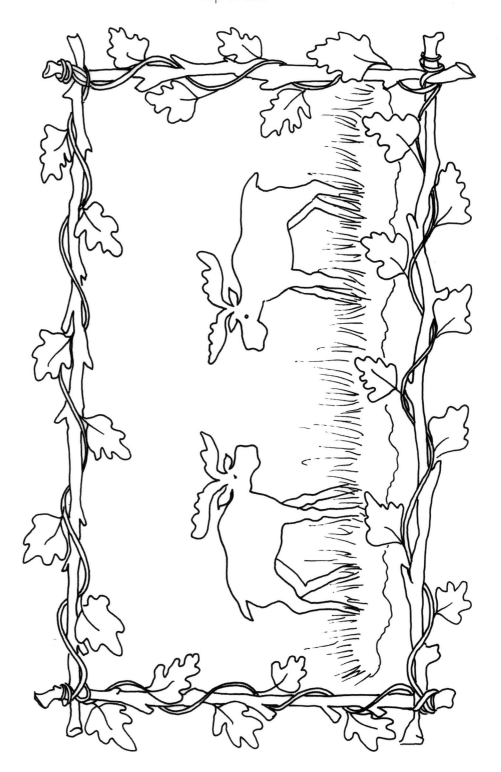

# PAINTING ON GLASS & CERAMIC SURFACES

## Preparation

Extensive preparation is unnecessary—simply put, the surface should be clean and dry before painting. Wiping the surface with rubbing alcohol before painting will remove any traces of grease or fingerprints.

## Types of Paint for Glass & Ceramics

**Acrylic enamels** are specially formulated to perform well when used on ceramics, glass, and tiles. These paints are self-sealing and scratch-resistant. They can be air dried to cure or baked in a home oven for added durability. When cured or baked, glass, china, porcelain, and tile are waterproof and top-shelf dishwasher safe; however, do not allow a painted piece to soak in water.

Do not mix water with acrylic enamels; instead, use mediums manufactured for use with the brand of paint you buy—flow medium for thinning, clear medium for floating, and extender for blending. (Water interferes with proper adhesion of the paint to the surface.) In the absence of flow medium, I have used one part water with two parts clear medium to make a thinning medium, but other than this type of thinning medium, stay away from water.

You can paint on glass and ceramic surfaces with **artist pigment acrylics** and **acrylic craft paints**, but the painted finish won't be as durable and the pieces can be used for decorative purposes only. Durability can be enhanced by using a sealer over the painted design. Also the paint sometimes has a tendency to bead up on the surface making strokework impossible.

## TIPS FOR WORKING WITH ACRYLIC ENAMELS

• Let the paint dry 30 minutes between coats.

• Work quickly because the paint dries quickly.

• Complete the painting within a 24-hour period. (This is for proper adhesion of the layers.)

• When finished, let the piece air dry to cure OR bake in your home oven, following the manufacturer's instructions. Don't touch the painted areas until the item has cooled completely; the paint remains soft until it cools.

*Pictured at right:* Lemon Cascade Glass Plate. Instructions begin on page 70.

# Lemon Cascade
## glass plate

*Pictured on page 68-69*

Sue Sensintaffar, who has been with me for many years, not only paints beautifully, she bakes beautifully. One of my favorite treats is her Lemon Bars. This project is my recipe for painting a wonderful plate on which to serve them.

Note: the paint is not food safe. If you wish to serve food on top of the painted area, place a clear glass plate on top of painted plate. You could also do a reverse painting technique. By painting the design *in reverse* on the back of a clear plate, you could serve on top of the plate.

## SUPPLIES

**Enamels for Glass:**

Burnt Sienna

Burnt Umber

Evergreen

Fresh Foliage

Lemon Custard

Warm White

**Brushes:**

Flats - #8, #10, #12, #14

Liner - #1

Wash - 1"

**Surface:**

Round glass plate, 14" dia.

**Other Supplies:**

*In addition to the Basic Painting Supplies listed on page 14, you'll need:*

Painting mediums for enamels

Glass etching compound

Dauber tool - 5/8"

Wax-free transfer paper

## PALETTE OF COLORS

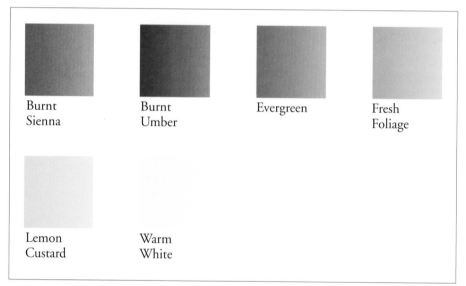

Burnt Sienna

Burnt Umber

Evergreen

Fresh Foliage

Lemon Custard

Warm White

## INSTRUCTIONS

**Prepare the Surface:**
1. Wash plate with soap and water. Dry thoroughly.
2. Following the manufacturer's instructions, carefully etch the plate with etching compound.
3. Neatly trace the design on tracing paper and transfer with wax-free transfer paper.

**Undercoat the Design:**
1. Undercoat the leaves with three coats of Fresh Foliage. Let the paint dry 30 minutes between each coat. (Photo 1, Fig. 1 on the Lemon Leaf Worksheet)
2. Undercoat the lemons with three coats of Lemon Custard. Let the paint dry 30 minutes between each coat. (Photo 1, Fig. 1 on Lemon Worksheet)

**Paint the Leaves - Option 1:**
*Two options for painting lemon leaves are illustrated. For option 1, see the Lemon Leaf Worksheet. For option 2, see photo series.*
1. Double load a flat brush with Burnt Umber and clear medium. Float shadows at the base as well as shadow areas of leaf. (A shadow area is the point at which one leaf goes behind another.) (Fig. 2) Let dry.

*Continued on page 72*

# Lemon Leaf Worksheet

Fig. 1

Fig. 2

Fig. 1 - Undercoat with three coats Fresh Foliage. Let the paint dry 30 minutes between coats.

Fig. 2 - Shade with floats of Burnt Umber.

Fresh Foliage

Warm White

Burnt Umber

Evergreen

Fig. 3

Fig, 4

Fig. 3 - Apply clear medium, then colors.

Fig. 4 - Blend.

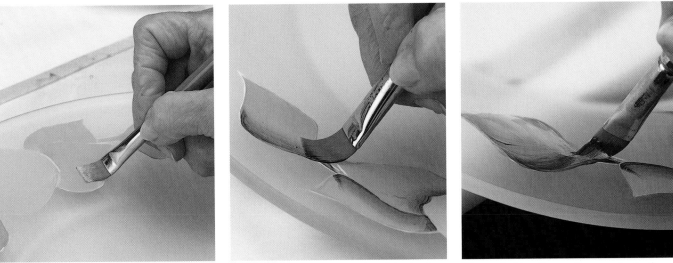

**Photo 1.** Undercoating.

**Photo 2.** Shading one side of the leaf.

**Photo 3.** Blending colors on the leaf.

*continued from page 70*

2. Working quickly, apply clear medium and colors (Warm White, Evergreen, Burnt Umber, and Fresh Foliage) to the leaf. (Fig. 3) Wipe the brush and blend lightly from base of leaf out and from outside edge back to base. (Fig. 4)

**Paint the Leaves - Option 2:**
*See the Photo Series of this option.*
1. Float a shadow of Evergreen at the base as well as shadow areas of leaf. (A shadow area is the point at which one leaf goes behind another.) (Photo 2) Let dry.
2. Working quickly, apply clear medium and colors to the leaf. I used Warm White and Fresh Foliage. Wipe the brush and blend lightly from base of leaf out and from outside edge back to base. (Photo 3)

**Paint the Lemons:**
*See The Lemon Worksheet.*
1. Double load your 1" wash brush with clear medium and Burnt Sienna. Blend on the palette to soften the color so it blends through the hairs of the brush from dark to medium to light. (Fig. 2) Float this on the dark side of the lemon. (Photo 4, Fig. 3) Let dry. A second and third coat may be floated, if desired, to deepen the shading.
2. Double load the brush with Fresh Foliage and clear medium. Shade the light side. (Photo 5, Fig. 3) Apply second and third coats, if needed. Be sure you allow the paint to dry between coats.
3. Dip the dauber in clear medium and blot on a soft, absorbent rag. Fill the dauber with Burnt Sienna and thoroughly blot it on the rag. Lightly pounce or dab the texture on the dark side of the lemon. (Photo 6, Figs. 4 and 5)
4. Dip the dauber in clear medium and blot on a soft, absorbent rag. Fill with Fresh Foliage and thoroughly blot it on the rag. Lightly pounce or dab the texture on the light side of the lemon. (Photo 7, Fig. 6)
5. *Option:* Flyspeck with a mixture of clear medium + Burnt Sienna (1:2).

**Curlicues:**
Mix Burnt Umber + Thicket (1:1). Use flow medium, **not water**, to thin the paint. Hold the handle of the brush so that it points straight up towards the ceiling. Slowly and deliberately paint the curlicues. *Option:* Let them dry and go back over a second and third time.

**Finish:**
Allow piece to cure or bake in a home oven according to the manufacturer's instructions. ❑

**Photo 4.** Shading one side of the lemon with Burnt Sienna.

**Photo 5.** Shading the other side of the lemon with Fresh Foliage.

**Photo 6.** Dabbing Burnt Sienna on the dark side of the lemon.

**Photo 7.** Dabbing Fresh Foliage on the other side.

# Lemon Worksheet

Fig. 2 - The float
(double loaded
Burnt Sienna and
clear medium)

Fig. 1 - Undercoat with three
coats Lemon Custard. Let
dry 30 minutes between
coats.

Fig. 3 - Float Burnt Sienna with a
1" brush. Let dry. Float Fresh
Foliage on the other side. Let dry.

Fig. 4 - Using a dauber
and clear medium,
pounce on Burnt Sienna.

Fig. 5 - Example of
pouncing with
Burnt Sienna.

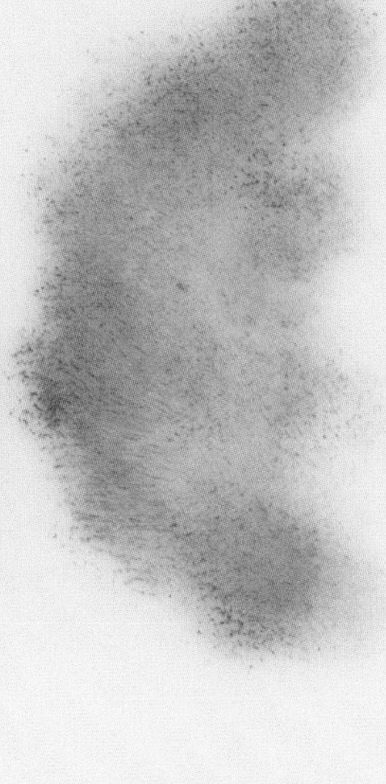

Fig. 6 - Using a dauber
and clear medium, pounce
on Fresh Foliage.

HAUSER

73

Left side

Right side

Pattern for Lemon
Cascade Glass Plate

(actual size)

*Instructions begin on
page 70.*

Pattern for Radishes Teapot Lamp

(actual size)

*Instructions begin on page 76.*

Lampshade borders

Bottom

Top

# Radishes
## teapot lamp

I love red and black, and I wanted red accents in my kitchen. This teapot lamp decorated with radishes hit the spot, so here it is.

The white china lamp, which I painted black except for a bit of white trim, is easy to paint with enamel paints especially designed for painting on china. Carefully follow the directions. You will be amazed at the results!

Acrylic craft paint was used to decorate the shade.

## TECHNIQUES TO LEARN:

Painting on china
Painting on black
Undercoating technique

## SUPPLIES

**Enamels for Glass:**

Autumn Leaves

Berry Wine

Engine Red

Fresh Foliage

Licorice

Thicket

Warm White

**Acrylic Craft Paint:**

Licorice

**Brushes:**

Flats - #6, #10, #12, 1"

Liner - #1

**Surface:**

China teapot lamp with white shade

**Other Supplies:**

*In addition to the Basic Painting Supplies listed on page 14, you'll need:*

Painting mediums for enamels

Rubbing alcohol

Wax-free transfer paper

*Pattern appears on page 75.*

## PALETTE OF COLORS

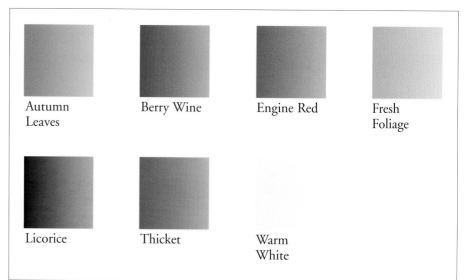

Autumn Leaves | Berry Wine | Engine Red | Fresh Foliage

Licorice | Thicket | Warm White

## INSTRUCTIONS

**Prepare the Surface:**

1. Carefully wash the china with soap and water. Dry thoroughly.
2. Wipe with rubbing alcohol.
3. Using a large flat brush, carefully paint the lamp base with Licorice enamel (**not** acrylic craft paint), leaving a white band around the lid. Let the paint dry and apply second coat, if needed. Let the paint dry and cure overnight.
4. Transfer the design using wax-free transfer paper.

**Paint the Radish:**

*See the Radish Worksheet.*

1. Undercoat the entire design with two coats of Warm White. (Photo 1, Fig. 1 on Radish Worksheet) Allow paint to dry 30 minutes between the coats or the paint will lift.
2. Mix Autumn Leaves + Engine Red (1:1). Under coat the radish area only with this mixture, letting a little bit of white show on the root. (Photo 2, Fig. 2) Let the paint dry 30 minutes.
3. Undercoat the radish tops with two coats of Fresh Foliage. (Photo 3, Fig. 2) Let dry 30 minutes between coats.

*Continued on page 78*

continued from page 76

4. Shade the radish with Berry Wine. (Photo 4, Fig. 2) Let dry 30 minutes.

5. Highlight the radish with Fresh Foliage + Warm White. (Photo 5, Fig. 2) Let the paint dry 30 minutes.

6. Shade the greenery with Thicket. (Photo 6, Fig. 2) Often I do this by double loading the brush with clear medium on one side and Thicket on the other. Float on the Thicket and don't go back over it—it will lift if you do! Let dry 30 minutes.

7. Highlight the greenery with Fresh Foliage and Warm White. (Fig. 3) Notice the S-stroke I used, stroking from the top of the foliage to the bottom. (There's an example on the worksheet.) Remember to let the paint dry 30 minutes between each coat. If you go back over it before that, the paint will lift.

8. Add line work, using the #1 liner brush and Berry Wine. (Fig. 3) (This carries a touch of the reddish color up into the foliage.) Let the paint dry and cure.

**Paint the Lamp Shade:**
*Use acrylic craft paint to paint the shade, **not** enamel.*

1. Carefully transfer the pattern and the word "Radishes" with gray graphite. If your graphite is new, rub it with a soft rag, so that there isn't such a dark transfer line. (That could really mess up the shade.)

2. Using your liner brush and/or a small flat brush with Licorice that has been thinned to a flowing consistency, paint the word and the border. Let dry.

**Finish:**
Allow the paint to cure for 21 days. (Then it can be wiped with water for cleaning purposes.) ❑

**Photo 1.** Undercoating with Warm White.

**Photo 2.** Undercoating with Autumn Leaves + Engine Red.

**Photo 3.** Undercoating with Fresh Foliage.

**Photo 4.** Floating shading with Berry Wine.

**Photo 5.** Floating highlights with Warm White + Fresh Foliage.

**Photo 6.** Floating shading on the greenery.

# Radish Worksheet

2 coats
Fresh Foliage

Shade with
Thicket

Fig. 1 -
Undercoat
with two
coats Warm
White.

Fig. 2 - Undercoat
and shade greenery,
and undercoat, shade,
and highlight the
radish.

2 coats red
mix (Autumn
Leaves +
Engine Red)

Shade with
Berry Wine

Highlight with
Fresh Foliage +
Warm White

Line work with
Berry Wine

Highlight with
Fresh Foliage +
Warm White

Fig. 3 - Highlight
greenery and add
line work.

# Three Types of Leaves
## tile trivets

I asked two of my dear friends and painting associates to create two of the trivets and I created the third one. Can you tell which one is mine?

The first trivet's design was stamped into modeling paste that was applied on the back (or rough side) of the tile. The second trivet's design was stamped with paint on the smooth side of the tile. (I used enamel paint for this one.) The third piece was created on the back (or rough side) of the tile which had been iced with modeling paste, then painted with a leaf design.

I know what you're wondering—can you put a hot plate on these trivets?

I don't think I would. I suggest they are for decorative purposes only; hang them on a wall and enjoy them.


## TECHNIQUES TO LEARN:

Paint on tile

Working with modeling paste

Stamping to create texture


## PALETTE OF COLORS

| Asphaltum | Burnt Sienna | Burnt Umber | Green Umber |
| Green Medium | Raw Sienna | Thicket | Turner's Yellow |
| Warm White | | | |

# Stamped Maple Leaf

## SUPPLIES

**Artist Pigment Acrylic Paints:**

Asphaltum

Green Umber

Raw Sienna

**Surface:**

Wood-framed tile trivet, holds 6" tiles

**Other Supplies:**

Palette knife

Soft rag

Wet palette

Flat artist brush, #12

Foam stamp - Maple leaf

Modeling paste

Glazing medium

Toothbrush

Waterbase varnish

## INSTRUCTIONS

**Prepare & Stamp:**

1. Using the palette knife, apply the modeling paste to the back of the tile as if you were icing a cake. (Photo 1)
2. Pick up the maple leaf foam stamp, press straight down firmly into the wet modeling paste (Photo 2), and lift straight up (Photo 3). Clean the stamp thoroughly, then stamp again. Repeat to fill the surface randomly with the stamped design. Let dry.

**Paint the Design:**

1. Mix Green Umber into glazing medium (1:2). Mix Raw Sienna and Asphaltum (1:2). Brush these colors generously on the tile (Photo 4), then wipe with a soft rag (Photo 5), allowing paint to remain in the crevices. Let dry.
2. Flyspeck with thinned Green Umber, using a toothbrush.

**Finish:**

Apply one or two coats waterbase varnish. ❑

**Photo 1.** Applying the modeling paste with a palette knife.

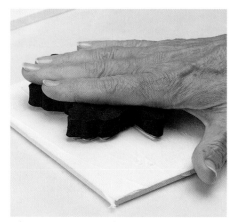

**Photo 2.** Pressing the stamp in the modeling paste.

**Photo 3.** Lifting the stamp.

**Photo 4.** Brushing paint over the stamped designs.

**Photo 5.** Wiping with a rag.

# Stamped Ash Leaf Trivet

## SUPPLIES

**Enamels for Glass:**

Burnt Sienna

Green Medium

Thicket

**Surface:**

Wood-framed tile trivet,
   holds 6" tiles

**Other Supplies:**

Painting medium

Foam stamp - Ash leaf

Toothbrush

Rubbing alcohol

Flat artist brush, #12

## INSTRUCTIONS

### Prepare the Surface:

1. Wash the tile with soap and water. Dry thoroughly.
2. Wipe with rubbing alcohol. Let dry.

### Stamp:

1. Brush Green Medium on the stamp, using a flat brush.
2. Stamp the tile, pressing straight down and lifting as many times as desired. Let dry. While the paint is drying, clean the sponge with water and dry it thoroughly.

3. Apply more Green Medium to one edge of the stamp. Re-stamp all the leaves to create a dark edge on each one. Let dry.
4. Flyspeck with Thicket, Burnt Sienna, and Green Medium. Use flow medium to thin the paint for fly-specking. ❑

# Painted Oak Leaf Trivet

## SUPPLIES

**Artist Pigment Acrylic Paints:**

Asphaltum

Burnt Umber

Green Umber

Turner's Yellow

Warm White

**Brushes:**

Flat - #10

Liner - #1

**Surface:**

Wood-framed tile trivet, holds 6" tiles

**Other Supplies:**

Sponge brush

Waterbase varnish

Modeling paste

Blending medium

Soft rags

Palette knife

Wet palette

*Pattern is on page 87.*

## INSTRUCTIONS

**Prepare:**

Apply modeling paste to the back of the tile using a palette knife, much as you would ice a cake. Let dry.

**Paint the Design:**

*See the Oak Leaf Worksheet.*

1. Using a large brush or a sponge brush, apply a wash of Green Umber.

2. Use a rag to wipe off some of the paint. Let dry.

3. Neatly trace and transfer the design.

4. Double load your large flat brush with Green Umber and water. Float around the outside edge of design. (Fig. 1) Let dry.

5. Float a Burnt Umber shadow at the base of the leaf. (Fig. 1) Let dry.

*Continued on page 87*

85

# Oak Leaf Worksheet

**The background shows the texture created by modeling paste, brought out by a Green Umber wash.**

Fig. 1 - Float Green Umber shading around the edge of the leaf. Float Burnt Umber at the base of the leaf.

Warm White

Fig. 2 - Apply colors

Turner's Yellow

Burnt Umber

Asphaltum

Fig. 3 - Blend. Paint veins with thinned Burnt Umber.

*Continued from page 85*

6. Apply a small amount of blending medium. Then, beginning at the bottom, apply Burnt Umber, Asphaltum, Turner's Yellow, and Warm White. (Fig. 2) Wipe your brush and quickly blend, using a light touch. (Fig. 3) Let the leaf dry.

7. Fill a number #1 liner brush with thinned Burnt Umber.

Paint the veins. (Fig. 3)

8. Flyspeck with thinned Burnt Umber and Asphaltum. Let dry.

**Finish:**

Varnish with two or more coats of waterbase varnish. ❑

## Pattern for Painted Oak Leaf Trivet

(actual size)

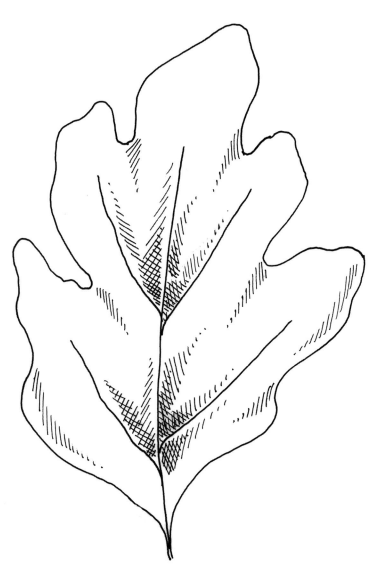

# Magical Dragonflies
## ceramic vase

At certain times of the year, in the panhandle of Florida along the Gulf of Mexico, the elegant dragonflies come sailing in—thousands of them. These majestic creatures have always fascinated me. They are mystical and magical, and they are gorgeous. You'll enjoy painting them on any surface, but isn't this china vase stunning? I used daubers in two sizes to paint the graduated segments of the dragonfly bodies.

## TECHNIQUES TO LEARN:

Painting on ceramics
Using a dauber tool to paint a design

## SUPPLIES

**Enamels for Glass:**

Berry Wine

Burnt Sienna

Gold

Italian Sage

Licorice

Sunflower

Wicker White

**Brushes:**

Flats - #4, #12

Liners - 2/0 #2

**Surface:**

Ceramic vase

**Other Supplies:**

*In addition to the Basic Painting Supplies listed on page 14, you'll need:*

Painting mediums for enamels

China marker *or* wax-free gray transfer paper

Daubers - 5/8" (large), 1/4" (small)

Rubbing alcohol

Cotton rags

*Pattern on page 93.*

## PALETTE OF COLORS

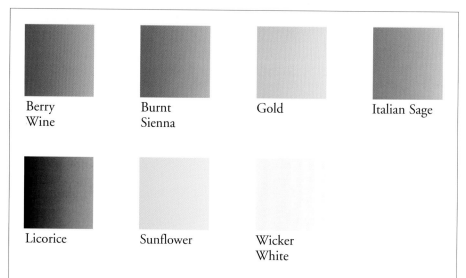

Berry Wine

Burnt Sienna

Gold

Italian Sage

Licorice

Sunflower

Wicker White

## INSTRUCTIONS

*See the Dragonfly Worksheet.*

**Prepare the Surface:**
1. Wash the vase with soap and water, rinse, and dry.
2. Wipe with alcohol. Let dry.
3. Neatly trace the pattern and transfer the design, using the wax-free paper or the china marker. To use the china marker, firmly go over the lines on the back of the design with the marker, then position the traced pattern on the surface with the china marker side against the surface and go over the pattern lines. The pattern will transfer to the surface.

**Undercoating the Body & Wings:**
1. Using long graceful strokes, undercoat the wings with Italian Sage. (Photo 1, Fig. 1)

*Continued on page 91*

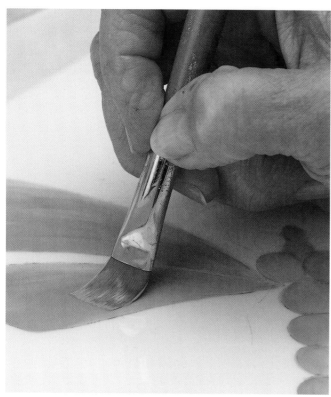

**Photo 1.** Undercoating the wings.

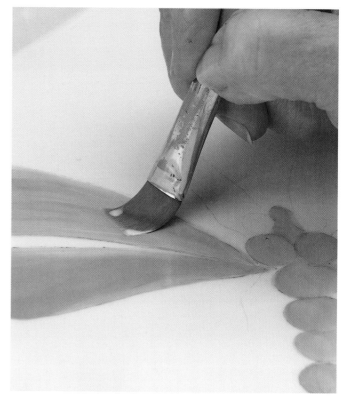

**Photo 2.** Washing Sunflower on the wings.

**Photo 3.** Shading with Berry Wine near the body.

**Photo 4.** Floating color on the edge of a wing.

*continued from page 88*

2. Dip the large dauber in clear medium and blot on a rag. Then dip in Italian Sage and blot thoroughly. Paint the body segments (Fig. 1), switching to the smaller dauber as you work towards the tail. Let the paint dry 30 minutes. A second coat may be applied, if desired.

## Paint the Wings:

1. Load a large flat brush with Sunflower + clear medium. Wash color on the outer areas of the wings and blend. (Photo 2, Fig. 2)
2. Double load the flat brush with Berry Wine and clear medium. Blend on the palette to soften colors, so that the color shades through the brush from dark to medium to light. Float color where the wings attach to the body (Photo 3, Fig. 2) and around the outside of the wing (Photo 4). Let the paint dry 30 minutes.
3. Using your liner brush, add details with Berry Wine. (Fig. 3) Let dry.
4. Outline, using your liner brush with Gold. (Photo 5, Fig. 3)

## Paint the Body:

1. Double load the dauber with Italian Sage and a touch of Burnt Sienna on the edge. Go back over the body to shade. (Photo 6, Fig. 2)

2. Repeat the technique on the light side, double loading the dauber with Italian Sage and Sunflower. (Fig. 3)
3. Using the liner brush, paint the lines between the circles with Burnt Sienna. (Fig. 3) Let dry.
4. Apply dots of Gold. (Fig. 3)
5. Mix Licorice + Burnt Sienna (1:2). Using the liner brush, neatly paint the legs and feelers. (Fig. 3)

## Paint the Eyes & "Nose":

1. Paint the eyes with Licorice. (Fig. 2) Let dry 30 minutes.
2. Highlight the eyes with dots of Warm White and tiny sloppy comma strokes of Gold. (Fig. 3)
3. Undercoat the "nose" with Italian Sage. (Fig. 1). Let dry.
4. Outline with Gold. (Fig. 3)

## Paint the Grass:

1. Using your #4 flat brush, undercoat the grass with Italian Sage. (Fig. 4) Let dry.
2. Overstroke with one coat of Sunflower. (Fig. 5) Let dry.
3. Float on some Berry Wine. (Fig. 6) Let dry. Add Sunflower highlights.

## Finish:

Let the piece air dry for 21 days *or* bake according to the paint manufacturer's instructions and let cool. ❑

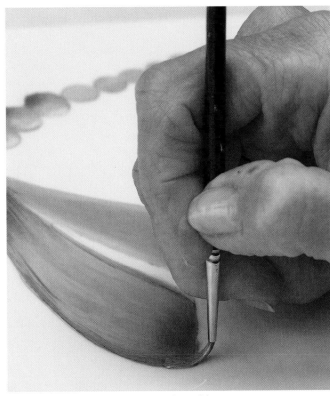

**Photo 5.** Outlining a wing with Gold.

**Photo 6.** Shading the body segments, using a dauber.

# Dragonfly Worksheet

Fig. 1 - Brush wings with Italian Sage to under-coat. Use daubers to paint the body segments.

Fig. 2 - Add colors.

Blend Berry Wine

Licorice

Blend Sunflower

Floats of Berry Wine

Burnt Sienna shading

Fig. 3 - Add details.

Gold outline

White dots

Gold highlights on eye and nose

Berry Wine details

Licorice + Burnt Sienna

Burnt Sienna

Sunflower highlighting

Gold dots

Fig. 4 - Brush grass with Italian Sage.

Fig. 5 - Pull Sunflower.

Fig. 6 - Shade with Berry Wine. Add Sunflower highlights.

Patterns for Magical Dragonflies Ceramic Vase
(Enlarge @200% for actual size.)

# Beautiful Butterflies
## candle lantern

Butterflies dance to the gentle, flickering glow of the candle on this wax candle lantern. The same enamel paints used for painting on glass and ceramics adhere well on the smooth surfaces of candles. To obtain the lush hues I wanted for the butterfly wings, I combined colors pre-mixed to make a crimson mix and a yellow mix. To further ensure good adhesion, I wipe the wax surface with rubbing alcohol before I start to paint.

## TECHNIQUES TO LEARN:

Painting on wax

## SUPPLIES

**Enamels for Glass:**

Autumn Leaves

Berry Wine

Burnt Umber

Butter Pecan

Engine Red

Sunflower

**Surface:**

Wax candle lantern

**Brushes:**

Flats - #2, #4, #8

Liner - #1

**Other Supplies::**

*In addition to the Basic Painting Supplies listed on page 14, you'll need:*

Rubbing alcohol

*Optional:* Clear matte acrylic sealer

*Pattern is on page 97.*

## PALETTE OF COLORS

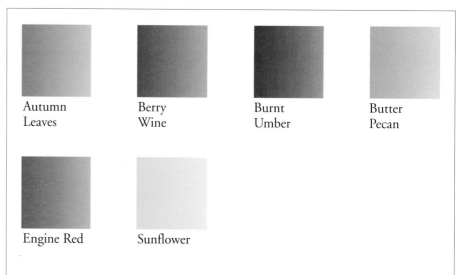

Autumn Leaves

Berry Wine

Burnt Umber

Butter Pecan

Engine Red

Sunflower

## INSTRUCTIONS

**Prepare the Surface:**

1. Wipe the candle with alcohol. Let dry.
2. Neatly trace and transfer your design, using gray graphite paper. *Option:* If the design doesn't stick, lightly spray your candle in a well-ventilated area with a quick coat of clear acrylic spray. Let dry. Then the pattern will transfer.

**Make Paint Mixes:**

1. For the crimson mix, combine Berry Wine + Autumn Leaves + Engine Red (3:1:1).
2. For the yellow mix, combine Butter Pecan + Sunflower (1:1).

**Paint the Small Butterfly:**

*See the Butterfly Worksheet.*

1. Paint the upper wings with the yellow mix, using long, gentle strokes. (Fig. 1)
2. Paint comma strokes on the lower portion of the wings with the crimson mix. Let dry 30 minutes. Apply a second coat, if desired. (Fig. 1)

*Continued on page 96*

# Butterfly Worksheet

Fig. 1 - Paint the small butterfly's wings with the crimson mix and the yellow mix.

Fig. 3 - Stroke upper portions of large butterfly's wings with a double loaded brush. Paint lower portions of wings with the crimson mix and the yellow mix.

Fig. 2 - Paint the body and antennae with Burnt Umber.

Fig. 4 - Paint the body and antennae with Burnt Umber. Add Burnt Umber outlines to lower portions of upper wings.

*continued from page 94*

3. Paint the body and antennae with Burnt Umber. Let dry 30 minutes. Apply a second coat, if desired. (Fig. 2)

**Paint the Large Butterfly:**
*See the Butterfly Worksheet.*

1. Double load the #8 flat brush with the yellow mix and the crimson mix. Blend on your palette and be sure the brush is good and full of paint. Paint a long, graceful comma stroke with the crimson color on the bottom.(Photo 1, Fig. 3)

2. Using the same double loaded brush, paint long slender U-strokes, three of four of them, making the strokes smaller as you progress down the wing. (Photo 2, Fig. 3)

3. Paint the lower portion of the upper wings with the yellow mix. Let dry 30 minutes.

4. Fill your #1 liner brush with Burnt Umber. Outline the lower part of the upper wings. (Fig. 4)
5. Paint the lower wings with the crimson mix and the yellow mix, using Fig. 4 of the Butterfly Worksheet as a guide for color placement. Let dry.
6. Paint the body and antennae with Burnt Umber. Let the paint dry and cure. ❏

## Patterns for Beautiful Butterflies Candle Lantern
### (actual size)

**Photo 1.** Painting a comma stroke with a double loaded brush.

**Photo 2.** Painting a U-stroke with a double loaded brush.

# PAINTING ON METAL

There are many different types of metal surfaces we can paint on: some are slick and shiny, others are more porous. Since many metal items are meant to be used outdoors, how and where an item will be used also should be part of the decision of which paint to use.

## Preparing Metal Surfaces

The preparation needed for metal items depends on the surface. Here are some guidelines:

*Items that have been primed or painted with a matte finish paint:* No preparation is required. Be sure the surface is clean and dry.

*Galvanized tin items:* Remove the oily film by wiping with a sponge and a solution of three parts water, one part vinegar. Don't immerse the piece in water—water can become trapped and cause problems later. Allow to dry thoroughly before painting.

*Painted, enameled, or slick surfaces:* Sponge with water and allow to dry.

*Rusty surfaces:* Sand with sandpaper to remove rust. If rust is especially heavy, consider using a commercial rust-remover and follow the manufacturer's instructions. Let dry completely. Spray with metal primer or sealer, then paint.

Metal pieces with a sprayed-on "rusty" finish are easy to paint on—the paint creates a good, workable painting surface that's an interesting background for painted designs. Rust-inhibiting primers are often this red-brown, rusty color.

## Types of Paint to Use on Metal

To paint on metal surfaces that are to be used indoors or outdoors, use **outdoor enamels** or weather-resistant indoor/outdoor paint. These paints are self-sealing and scratch-resistant. They do not need to be sealed after paint is dry and they are fade resistant.

Do not mix water with acrylic enamels; instead, use mediums manufactured for use with the brand of paint you buy—flow medium for thinning, clear medium for floating, and extender for blending. (Water interferes with the proper adhesion of the paint to the surface.)

You also can use **artist pigment acrylic** and **acrylic craft paints** on metal items. After the paint has dried and cured, apply several coats of varnish (choose an outdoor varnish for items to be used outdoors). I like to apply a coat of paste wax over the final coat of varnish.

*Pictured left:* Daisy Bouquet Watering Can. Instructions begin on next page.

# Daisy Bouquet
## watering can

*Pictured on page 98-99*

This is one of my favorites, I just love the combination of the white and yellow daisies on the soft blue background—it's clean, bright, and happy. It can be used in any number of places as a decorative accessory. I added comma strokes on the spout to coordinate with the punched design around the top of my can. If your can doesn't have the cutouts, you could add a painted design there as well. Because I wanted to use it inside as a decorative accessory, I used artist pigment acrylics. Use outdoor enamel paints if you plan to use outdoors.

## TECHNIQUES TO LEARN:

Painting on metal

Painting strokework daisies

## SUPPLIES

**Artist Pigment Acrylic Paints:**

Burnt Sienna          Green Dark

Green Light           Green Medium

Green Umber           Medium Yellow

Payne's Gray          Titanium White

Warm White

**Acrylic Craft Paint:**

Pure Gold (metallic)

**Brushes:**

Flat - #6

Filbert - #6

Liner or scroller - #1

Wash - 1"

**Surface:**

Pale blue watering can

**Other Supplies:**

*In addition to the Basic Painting Supplies listed on page 14, you'll need:*

Rust-preventive primer

Pale blue spray paint

Blending medium

Glazing medium

Gloss spray sealer

## PALETTE OF COLORS

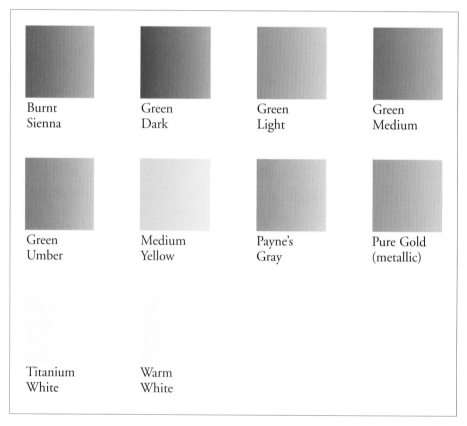

Burnt Sienna

Green Dark

Green Light

Green Medium

Green Umber

Medium Yellow

Payne's Gray

Pure Gold (metallic)

Titanium White

Warm White

## INSTRUCTIONS

**Prepare the Surface:**

1. *If your watering can is already painted,* wash with soap and water. Dry thoroughly. *If your watering can is NOT painted,* spray with primer. Let dry and cure. Following manufacturer's instructions, spray with baby blue spray paint. Let dry thoroughly.
2. Neatly trace and carefully transfer using white or gray graphite paper.

*Continued on page 102*

# Scribble Leaf Worksheet

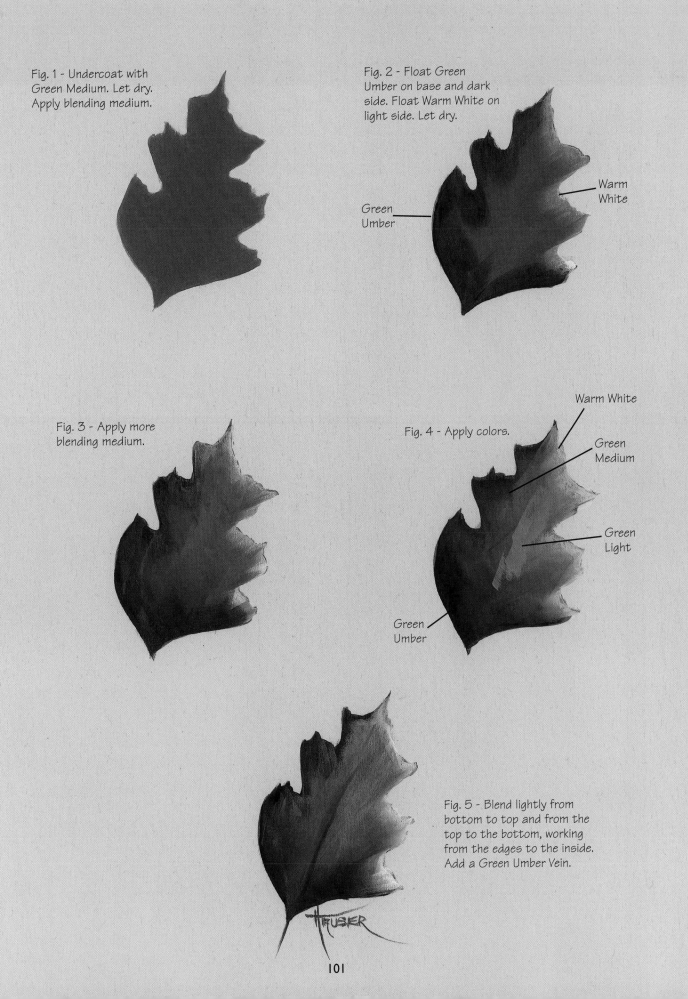

Fig. 1 - Undercoat with Green Medium. Let dry. Apply blending medium.

Fig. 2 - Float Green Umber on base and dark side. Float Warm White on light side. Let dry.

Green Umber

Warm White

Fig. 3 - Apply more blending medium.

Fig. 4 - Apply colors.

Warm White

Green Medium

Green Light

Green Umber

Fig. 5 - Blend lightly from bottom to top and from the top to the bottom, working from the edges to the inside. Add a Green Umber Vein.

TRUSKER

101

continued from page 100

**Paint the Background:**

Double load a very large flat brush with just a little Payne's Gray and glazing medium. Blend on the palette to soften color. Lightly pat or gently stroke this around the outside edge of the design. (This creates a soft shadow behind your painting.)

**Paint the Leaves:**

*See the Scribble Leaf Worksheet.*

1. Undercoat the leaves with Green Medium. (Two or three coats will be needed to cover.) (Photo 1, Fig. 1) Let the paint dry between each coat, then let the final coat cure for two or three days.
2. Apply a little blending medium to the leaf. Double load the brush with blending medium and Green Umber. Float Green Umber on at the base of the leaf and down the dark side. (Photo 2, Fig. 2) "Scribble" the brush to fill in the dark side of the leaf. (Photo 3)
3. Double load the brush with blending medium and Warm White. Apply the Warm White to the light side of the leaf, scribbling again. (Photo 4, Fig. 2) Let dry.
4. Apply a little more blending medium. (Fig. 3) Apply colors (Green Umber, Warm White, Green Medium, and Green Light). (Photo 5, Fig. 4) Wipe the brush. Blend from the base up and from the outside edges back to the base, using a very light touch. (Photo 6, Fig. 5)
5. Apply a Green Umber vein. (Fig. 5)

**Paint the White Daisy:**

The technique for painting white daisies and yellow daisies is exactly the same—only the colors are different. Daisies can be painted with round, flat or filbert brushes. I have chosen a #6 filbert.

*See the Daisy Worksheet. If necessary, to keep the paint wet, work one petal or section of petals at a time.*

1. Apply a little blending medium to the petals, carefully— not too much. Undercoat the petals with Payne's Gray, stroking from the outside edge towards the center. (Fig. 1)

**Photo 1.** Undercoating a leaf.

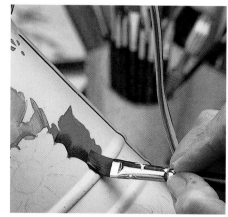

**Photo 2.** Floating a shadow on the dark side.

**Photo 3.** "Scribbling" color on the dark side.

**Photo 4.** "Scribbling" color on the light side.

**Photo 5.** Adding colors to the center.

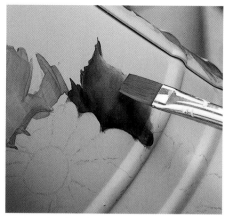

**Photo 6.** Blending the colors.

2. Wipe the brush and pick of Titanium White. Starting at the outside edge of the undercoat color while it is wet, apply comma strokes over the Payne's Gray. (Figs. 1 and 2) Let dry.

3. To deepen the color at the center, double load a large flat brush with Payne's Gray and water. Float Payne's Gray at the base of each petal where it would touch the center. (Fig. 2)

4. Undercoat the center with Titanium White. (Fig. 6) Let dry.

5. Undercoat with Medium Yellow. (Fig. 7) Let dry.

6. Double load the brush with Medium Yellow and Burnt Sienna. Blend on the palette to soften the color. Float the dark shading down the left side and across the bottom of the center. (Fig. 3)

7. Using the #1 liner brush and thinned paint, apply dots of Payne's Gray and Titanium White. (Fig. 3) TIP: Please study the application of the dots on the worksheet. Don't line them up like mouse tracks. Let some of the dots fall into the center and others out on the petals. The purpose of the dots, besides creating beauty, is to visually attach the petals to the center.

**Photo 7.** Undercoat the petals with Burnt Sienna.

**Photo 9.** Shading the center with Burnt Sienna.

**Photo 8.** Overstroking the petals with Medium Yellow.

**Photo 10.** Applying dots of Burnt Sienna around the center.

**Paint the Yellow Daisy:**

*See the Daisy Worksheet. If necessary, to keep the paint wet, work one petal or section of petals at a time.*

1. Apply a little blending medium to the petals, carefully—not too much. Undercoat the petals with Burnt Sienna, stroking from the outside edge towards the center. (Photo 7, Fig. 4)

2. Wipe the brush and pick of Medium Yellow. Starting at the outside edge of the undercoat color while it is wet, apply comma strokes over the Burnt Sienna. (Photo 8, Figs. 4 and 5) Let dry.

3. To deepen the color at the center, double load a large flat brush with Burnt Sienna and water. Float Burnt Sienna at the base of each petal where it would touch the center. (Fig. 5)

4. Undercoat the center with Titanium White. (Fig. 6) Let dry.

5. Undercoat in Medium Yellow. (Fig. 7) Let dry.

6. Double load the brush with Medium Yellow and Burnt Sienna. Blend on the palette to soften the color. Float the dark shading down the left side and across the bottom of the center. (Photo 9, Fig. 8)

7. Using the #1 liner brush and thinned paint, apply dots of Burnt Sienna and Titanium White. (Photo 10, Fig. 8) TIP: Please study the application of the dots on the worksheet. Don't line them up like mouse tracks. Let some of the dots fall into the center and others out on the petals. The purpose of the dots, besides creating beauty, is to visually attach the petals to the center.

*Continued on page 105*

# Daisy Worksheet

**White Daisy:**

Fig. 1 - Apply blending medium to petals. Understroke with Payne's Gray.

Fig. 2 - Overstroke with Titanium White. Let dry. Float Payne's Gray on each petal where the petal touches the center.

Payne's Gray + water

Fig. 3 - Paint center. (See below.) Apply dots of Payne's Gray and Titanium White.

Fig. 4 - Apply blending medium to petals. Understroke with Burnt Sienna. Overstroke with Medium Yellow.

**Yellow Daisy:**

Fig. 5 - Shade petals around the center with floats of Burnt Sienna. Paint center. (See below.) Apply dots of Burnt Sienna and Titanium White.

**Daisy Center:**

Fig. 6 - Undercoat with Titanium White. Let dry.

Fig. 7 - Paint with Medium Yellow. Shade with Burnt Sienna.

Fig. 8 - Apply dots. (Here, Burnt Sienna and Titanium White.)

*continued from page 103*

**Paint the Stems:**

1. Paint the stems with Green Medium.
2. Shade the dark sides with Green Dark or Green Umber.
3. Highlight the light sides with a bit of Warm White. Let dry.
4. Double load a flat brush and float shadows where the stems go behind the daisies.

**Paint the Trim:**

1. Trim the edges of the watering can with Pure Gold. Let dry and cure.
2. Paint the comma strokes on the spout with Green Dark.

**Finish:**

Spray with two or more coats of satin varnish. ❑

Pattern for Daisy Bouquet Watering Can

(actual size)

# Grape Harvest
## metal party tub

Painting on metal pieces is a quick, easy, and extremely effective way to create interesting tabletop accessories. This wonderful tub can be filled with flowers for a unique centerpiece or filled with ice to cool sodas or wine. However you choose to use it, it will add class and charm to your table.

My bucket had a painted finish when I bought it, but you could use a galvanized tin bucket and apply a basecoat with spray paint. I used a dauber to paint the round grapes—it's fun and easy. For best results, I suggest you practice using the dauber on an old piece of wood before painting the tub. You'll see step by step examples on the Grapes Worksheet in this section.

### TECHNIQUES TO LEARN:

Using a dauber to paint grapes

*Instructions begin on page 108.*

# Grape Harvest
## metal party tub

*Pictured on page 106-107*

## SUPPLIES

**Outdoor Enamel Paints:**

Green Dark

Green Light

Green Medium

Green Umber

Prussian Blue

Pure Magenta

Warm White

**Brushes:**

Flats - #10, #14, #16, #20

Liner - #1

**Surface:**

Painted metal tub

**Other Supplies:**

*In addition to the Basic Painting Supplies listed on page 14, you'll need:*

Blending medium

Dauber, 5/8"

*Pattern is on page 111.*

## PALETTE OF COLORS

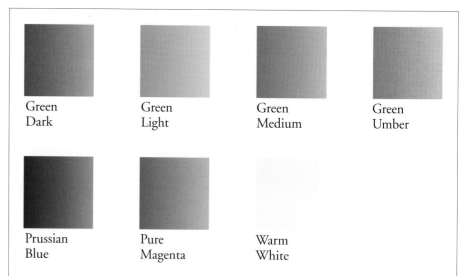

Green Dark

Green Light

Green Medium

Green Umber

Prussian Blue

Pure Magenta

Warm White

## INSTRUCTIONS

**Prepare the Surface:**

1. Wash the bucket with soap and water. Dry thoroughly.
2. Neatly trace the design and transfer with white transfer paper.

**Paint the Leaves:**

*See The Grapes Worksheet.*

1. Neatly and carefully undercoat the leaves with two or more coats Green Dark (Fig. 1) or Green Medium. (If you're painting on a dark surface, using a lighter base color affords more contrast.) Let the paint dry and cure between the coats. NOTE: Before continuing, let the paint dry 48 hours. IF you don't, it will easily lift off the metal background.
2. Float a shadow at the base of the leaf and along one side with Green Umber. (Photo 1) Let dry thoroughly.
3. Apply a thin coat of blending medium. Apply the colors—Green Umber, Green Medium, Warm White, and (if you wish) a little Green Light. (Photo 2, Fig. 2) Quickly blend from the base of the leaf out, and from the outside edge back. (Photo 3, Fig. 3) Don't overwork this or the paint could lift.
4. Using your #1 liner brush with Green Umber, paint the veins. (Fig. 3)

**Paint the Grapes:**

1. Dip the dauber in blending medium (Photo 4) and blot on a soft cotton rag or towel (Photo 5). Fill the dauber with Prussian Blue (Photo 6) and blot several times. (You don't want too much paint in the dauber.) Paint all the grapes with Prussian Blue (Fig. 5).

*Continued on page 110*

**Photo 1.** Floating shading on a leaf.

**Photo 2.** Applying color to a leaf.

**Photo 3.** Blending.

**Photo 4.** Dipping the dauber in blending medium.

**Photo 5.** Blotting the dauber on a towel.

**Photo 6.** Picking up color on the

**Photo 7.** Adding some Green Light to the dauber.

**Photo 8.** Blotting the dauber on the palette.

**Photo 9.** Pressing the dauber on the bucket surface.

# Grapes Worksheet

**Grape Leaves:**

Fig. 1 - Undercoat with Green Dark.

Fig. 2 - Float shading with Green Umber. Let dry. Add blending medium and colors.

Warm White

Green Medium

Green Umber

Fig. 3 - Blend. Add vein.

**Purple Grapes:**

Fig. 4 - Colors for purple grapes

Prussian Blue + Warm White

More Warm White

Prussian Blue

Prussian Blue + Pure Magenta

Fig. 5 - Dark value grapes

Fig. 6 - Adding medium value grapes

Fig. 7 - Adding light value grapes

Fig. 8 - One grape accented with Green Light

*continued from page 108*

2. Pick up a bit of Pure Magenta on the edge of the dauber. Paint the medium value grapes (Fig. 6).
3. Make a light blue mix of Warm White + Prussian Blue (3:1). Pick up a touch of this highlight color on the edge of the dauber. Highlight your medium value grapes with the light blue mix, pressing straight down and gently turning the dauber just slightly from side to side (Fig. 7).
4. To paint the light grapes, pick up more Warm White (Fig. 4) or some Green Light (Fig. 8) on the edge of the dauber (Photo 7). Blot on your palette or the rag (Photo 8) and press to the surface to paint just a few light grapes (Photo 9).

**Paint the Stems:**

1. Paint the stems with Green Medium.
2. Shade with Green Umber.

**Finish:**

To paint the curlicues, fill the #1 liner brush with a thinned mix of Green Medium + Green Light (1:1). (Remember the brush must be full of thinned paint.) Hold the handle of the liner brush so that it points straight up to the ceiling and paint the curlicues. Let the piece dry and cure. ❏

Pattern for Grape Harvest Party Tub

(Enlarge @200% for actual size)

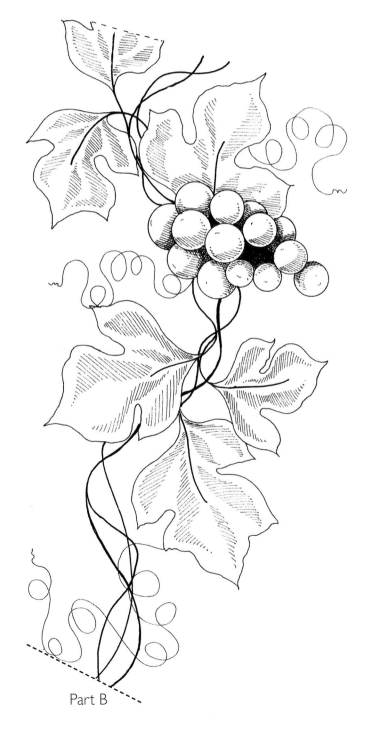

Part A

Part B

# PAINTING
# ON
# FABRIC

Tote bags, pillows, tablecloths, and napkins are just a few of the
surfaces that can be embellished with decorative painting.

## Preparation

If you wish to wash an item after you've painted it, you'll want to wash and dry
the item according to the manufacturer's instructions before painting. Press with
an iron to smooth the surface and remove any wrinkles. Washing also removes
sizing and other fabric finishes that could interfere with paint adhesion.

## Types of Paint to Use

For permanent, washable painted designs on fabrics, use **textile medium** with
**artist pigment acrylic** or **acrylic craft paints**. Choose a textile medium that's the
same brand as your paint and follow the package instructions or this basic
guideline: simply mix the paint colors with an equal amount of textile medium
before beginning to paint.

*Pictured right:* Summer Geraniums Canvas Tote. Project begins on page 114.

# Summer Geraniums
## canvas tote

*Pictured on page 113*

Take a plain canvas bag and create a masterpiece with just a little bit of paint and trim; your tote will become a treasure. When painting on fabric, it is customary to wash the piece before painting; however, to preserve the bag's crisp appearance, I did not wash it before painting. Spot clean as needed.

## TECHNIQUES TO LEARN:

Painting on fabric
Painting geraniums
Lettering technique

## SUPPLIES

**Artist Pigment Acrylic Paints:**

Burnt Sienna
Green Dark
Green Light
Green Medium
Red Light
True Burgundy
Warm White
Yellow Light

**Acrylic Craft Paint:**

Licorice

**Brushes:**

Wash - 1"
Filbert - #4
Flats - #4, #8, #10, #12

**Surface:**

Canvas tote bag

**Other Supplies:**

*In addition to the Basic Painting Supplies listed on page 14, you'll need:*

Textile medium
Black ball fringe trim or other trim
Needle and black thread *or* fabric glue

## PALETTE OF COLORS

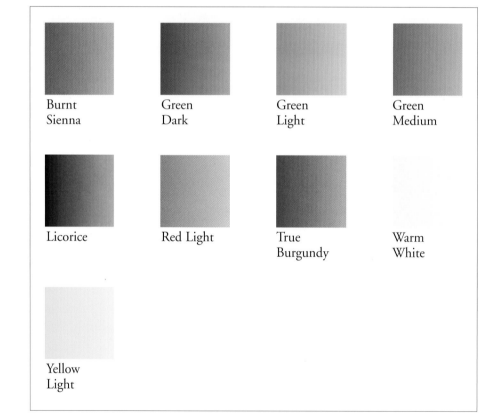

Burnt Sienna

Green Dark

Green Light

Green Medium

Licorice

Red Light

True Burgundy

Warm White

Yellow Light

*Instructions begin on page 117.*

# Geranium Worksheet

Fig. 1 - Paint rectangle with Licorice. Let dry. Transfer the design.

Fig. 2 - Apply textile medium. Stroke petals with True Burgundy.

Green Medium stems

Fig. 3 - Overstroke some petals with Red Light. Shade stems with Green Dark.

True Burgundy

Red Light

Fig. 4 - Add lightest flowers with Red Light + Warm White (3:1). Dot centers with Medium Yellow, then Licorice.

**Photo 1.** Applying textile medium to a leaf.

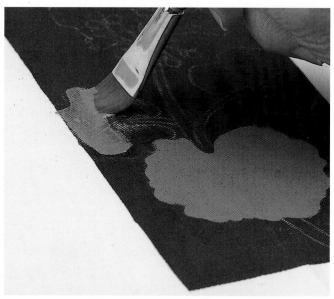

**Photo 2.** Undercoating a leaf with Green Medium.

**Photo 3.** Applying more textile medium to the leaf over the undercoat.

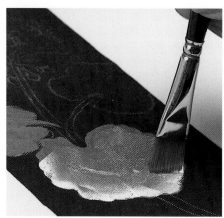

**Photo 4.** Floating Warm White on a leaf.

**Photo 5.** Stroking with Burnt Sienna.

**Photo 6.** Applying color to the leaf.

**Photo 7.** Blending to pull down the Burnt Sienna.

continued from page 114

## INSTRUCTIONS

### Prepare the Surface:

*See the Geranium Worksheet.*

1. Transfer the rectangle to the tote with gray graphite.
2. Using the large flat brush, paint the rectangle with one or two coats Licorice. (Fig. 1) Let dry thoroughly.
3. Using white graphite paper, transfer the design. (Fig. 1)

### Paint the Geraniums:

*See the Geranium Worksheet.*

1. Apply textile medium to the clump of geraniums. (Photo 8)
2. With True Burgundy, paint five-petal flowers all over the clump. Be sure you have very uneven, staggered edges—you don't want your geraniums to look like red hydrangeas. (Fig. 2, Photo 9)
3. While the paint is wet, pick up Red Light. Paint a few Red Light flowers over the True Burgundy. (Fig. 3, Photo 10)
4. While the paint is still wet, with a mixture of Red Light + Warm White (3:1), paint just a few light flowers here and there. (Fig. 4, Photo 11)

### Paint the Flower Centers:

1. Using your liner brush with thinned paint, apply a dot of Medium Yellow in the very center of the flower. (Fig. 4, Photo 12)

*Continued on page 119*

**Photo 8.** Applying textile medium to the flower cluster.

**Photo 9.** Applying strokes of True Burgundy to create flowers.

**Photo 10.** Overstroking some petals with Red Light.

**Photo 11.** Adding the lightest flower petals.

**Photo 12.** Dotting the centers with Medium Yellow.

# Geranium Worksheet

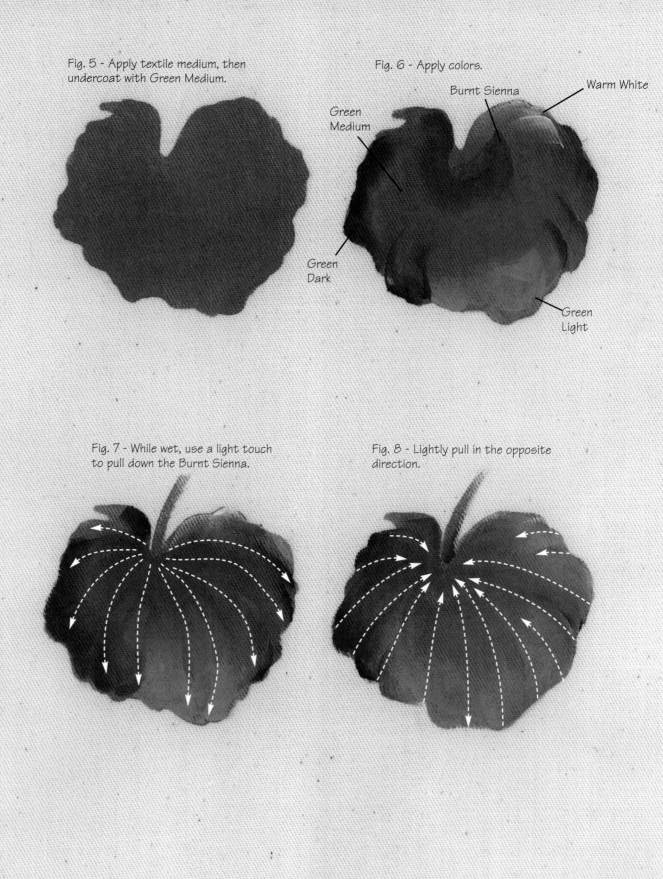

Fig. 5 - Apply textile medium, then undercoat with Green Medium.

Fig. 6 - Apply colors.

Green Medium

Burnt Sienna

Warm White

Green Dark

Green Light

Fig. 7 - While wet, use a light touch to pull down the Burnt Sienna.

Fig. 8 - Lightly pull in the opposite direction.

*continued from page 117*

2. Apply a tiny dot of Licorice on top of the yellow. (Fig. 4)

**Paint the Stems:**

1. Using the liner brush or the chisel edge of a small flat brush, paint the stems with Green Medium. (Fig. 2)
2. Shade with Green Dark. (Fig. 3) Be sure to paint dark shadows where stems go underneath the flowers.
3. *Option:* Highlight with Warm White.

**Paint the Buds:**

1. Paint the buds with Red Light. (Fig. 3)
2. Shade at the base with a touch of True Burgundy. (Fig. 3)
3. Add bracts with Green Medium + Green Dark. (Fig. 4)

**Paint the Geranium Leaves:**

1. Apply textile medium (Photo 1). Undercoat the leaf with Green Medium (Fig. 5, Photo 2).
2. While wet, shade the edge with Green Dark. (Fig. 6)
3. Apply textile medium again (Photo 3), then float Warm White (Photo 4). Paint a rather large U-stroke towards the top of the leaf with Burnt Sienna. (Fig. 6, Photo 5) Add Green Light to the leaf (Photo 6).
4. Quickly wipe the brush and pull the Burnt Sienna into the Green. (Fig. 7, Photo 7)
5. Wipe your brush again. Using a light touch, pull the Green Light back up towards the Burnt Sienna. (Fig. 8)

**Finish:**

1. Use a small flat brush to paint the word "Geranium" on the front of the bag.
2. Glue or stitch on the ball fringe. ❑

## Pattern for Summer Geraniums Canvas Tote

(actual size)

# Painting on Paper

*A handpainted greeting card or invitation is a gift in itself and a wonderful way to share your love of painting.*

## Paints for Paper

**Paper paints** are designed to work on just about any paper. You can add wonderful color, dimension, and accents to cards with paper paints.

Dimensional paper paints come in squeeze bottles with applicator tips, so they're easy to use for embellishing and writing. They can be used to create dimensional, textured, or flat finishes. You can thin this paint with a clear medium made specifically for it and use it for brush painting or use more medium and use the thinned paint like a wash.

They are acid free and, when dry, won't stick to other paper surfaces. They are flexible and won't crack as the paper bends, making them perfect for cards that will be mailed, and they don't distort the paper.

**Artist pigment acrylic** and **acrylic craft paints** can be used for painting on paper as well. They work best on stiffer papers (like cards or envelopes that will contain cards) and smooth finish papers.

*Pictured right:* Sweet Violets Greeting Card. Instructions begin on page 122.

# Sweet Violets
## greeting card

When you have learned to paint brush strokes and simple leaves, you will have a lot of fun painting little bouquets of flowers. This greeting card, with its bouquet of handpainted violets, makes a wonderful, frame-able gift.

## TECHNIQUES TO LEARN:

Painting on paper
Strokework violets
Using decorative punches

## SUPPLIES

**Artist Pigment Acrylic Paints or Paper Paints:**

Dioxazine Purple

Green Medium

Green Umber

Medium Yellow

Payne's Gray

Red Light

Warm White

**Acrylic Craft Paints or Paper Paints:**

Bayberry

Heather

**Brushes:**

Flats - #1, #4, #10, #12

Liner - #1

*Optional:* Filbert - #4

**Surface:**

Matte finish greeting card with envelope

**Other Supplies:**

*In addition to the Basic Painting Supplies listed on page 14, you'll need:*

Blending medium

Corner punch ·

## PALETTE OF COLORS

Bayberry

Dioxazine Purple

Green Medium

Green Umber

Heather

Medium Yellow

Payne's Gray

Red Light

Warm White

## INSTRUCTIONS

**Prepare:**

1. Neatly trace the design. Transfer the design with gray graphite transfer paper, using a light touch.
2. Make mix #1 - Warm White + a touch of Payne's Gray + Dioxazine Purple. See the Violets Worksheet, Fig. 14.

**Paint the Leaves:**

*The leaves should be painted first because they are underneath the violets.*

1. Undercoat the leaves with two coats of Bayberry. (Fig. 1) Let the paint dry between each coat.
2. Anchor the base of each leaf with a float of Green Umber. (Fig. 2)

3. Apply blending medium to the entire leaf. While wet, double load your #10 or #12 flat brush with Green Umber and Green Medium. Blend on the palette to soften the color. Reapply the shadow at the base of the leaf, then stroke the dark side of the leaf. (Fig. 3)

4. Double load the brush with Green Medium and Warm White. Apply the strokes to the light side of the leaf. (Fig. 4)

5. Wipe the brush and quickly apply a touch of Green Medium and Warm White to the center. (Fig. 4)

6. Wipe the brush and blend from the base of the leaf out into the strokes, then from the outside edge back to the base. (Fig. 5) Careful—don't overblend. Let dry.

7, Accent with a float of Payne's Gray at the base. (Fig. 6)

## Paint the Violet:

1. Using the small flat brush or filbert (your choice), neatly undercoat the violet petals with Heather. (Fig. 7) Let dry.

2. Carefully overstroke with mix #1. (Fig. 8)

3. Shade the petals at the center with a float of Dioxazine Purple + Payne's Gray (1:1). (Fig. 9)

4. Carefully paint the triangular center with Medium Yellow. (Fig. 10, Fig. 11)

5. With a tiny liner, paint two comma-like strokes of Warm White. (Fig. 10, Fig. 12)

6. Paint a tiny dot of Red Light in the throat of the triangle. (Fig. 10, Fig. 13) Let dry.

## Paint the Bud:

1. Undercoat the blossom petals of the bud with Heather. (Fig. 15)

2. Undercoat the leaves, calyx, and stems with Bayberry. (Fig. 15)

3. Shade the leaves, calyx, and stems with Green Umber. (Fig. 16)

4. Overstroke the bud with mix #1. (Fig. 16)

5. Float on the Payne's Gray + Dioxazine Purple mix at the center. (Fig. 17)

6. Highlight with Warm White. (Fig. 17)

## Paint the Stems:

1. Paint the stems with Bayberry. (Fig. 15)

2. Shade with Green Umber. (Fig. 16)

3. Highlight with Warm White. (Fig. 17)

## Finish:

1. Thin the dark mix (Dioxazine Purple + Payne's Gray (1:1)) and paint the curlicues and a thin bow around the stems. Let dry.

2. Punch the lower corners of the card with the punch. (Photo 1)

3. Open the card. (Photo 2) On the inside, carefully paint the corners with mix #1. Let dry.

4. *Optional:* Paint a blossom on the back of the envelope. ❏

**Photo 1:** Punch lower corners of the card with the punch.

**Photo 2:** Open card and paint the corners.

# Violets Worksheet

Fig. 7 - Undercoat with Heather.

Fig. 8 - Overstroke with mix #1.

Fig. 9 - Float with Dioxazine Purple + Payne's Gray (1:1).

Fig. 10 - Paint center.

Fig. 11 - Medium Yellow center

Fig. 12 - Comma strokes of Warm White

Fig. 13 - Red Light dot

Fig. 14 - Mix #1

Fig. 15 - Undercoat blossom with Heather and leaves and stem with Bayberry.

Fig. 16 - Overstroke petals with mix #1. Shade leaf with Green Umber.

Fig. 17 - Shade petals with Dioxazine Purple + Payne's Gray. Highlight stem and leaf with Warm White.

Fig. 1 - Undercoat with Bayberry. Let dry.

Fig. 2 - Anchor the base with a Green Umber float.

Fig. 3 - Apply blending medium. Stroke base and dark side with Green Umber and Green Medium.

Fig. 4 - Stroke light side with Green Medium and Warm White. Add the colors to the center.

Fig. 5 - Blend from the bottom up and the top down.

Fig. 6 - Let dry. Accent the base with a Payne's Gray float.

Pattern for Sweet Violets Greeting Card

(actual size)

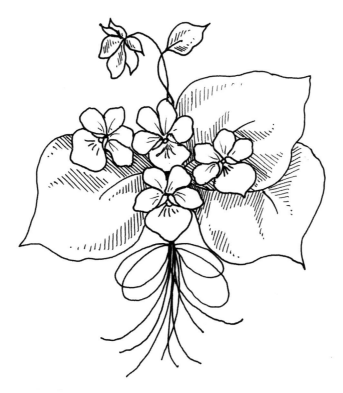

# METRIC CONVERSION CHART

## Inches to Millimeters and Centimeters

| Inches | MM | CM |
|--------|-----|------|
| 1/8 | 3 | .3 |
| 1/4 | 6 | .6 |
| 3/8 | 10 | 1.0 |
| 1/2 | 13 | 1.3 |
| 5/8 | 16 | 1.6 |
| 3/4 | 19 | 1.9 |
| 7/8 | 22 | 2.2 |
| 1 | 25 | 2.5 |
| 1-1/4 | 32 | 3.2 |
| 1-1/2 | 38 | 3.8 |
| 1-3/4 | 44 | 4.4 |
| 2 | 51 | 5.1 |
| 3 | 76 | 7.6 |
| 4 | 102 | 10.2 |
| 5 | 127 | 12.7 |
| 6 | 152 | 15.2 |
| 7 | 178 | 17.8 |
| 8 | 203 | 20.3 |
| 9 | 229 | 22.9 |
| 10 | 254 | 25.4 |
| 11 | 279 | 27.9 |
| 12 | 305 | 30.5 |

## Yards to Meters

| Yards | Meters |
|-------|--------|
| 1/8 | .11 |
| 1/4 | .23 |
| 3/8 | .34 |
| 1/2 | .46 |
| 5/8 | .57 |
| 3/4 | .69 |
| 7/8 | .80 |
| 1 | .91 |
| 2 | 1.83 |
| 3 | 2.74 |
| 4 | 3.66 |
| 5 | 4.57 |
| 6 | 5.49 |
| 7 | 6.40 |
| 8 | 7.32 |
| 9 | 8.23 |
| 10 | 9.14 |

# INDEX

*Continued on next page*

# INDEX (Continued)